PREDICAMENTS

Moral Difficulty in Everyday Life

Robert A. Stebbins
The University of Calgary

UNIVERSITY
PRESS OF
AMERICA

Lanham • New York • London

Copyright © 1993 by
University Press of America®, Inc.
4720 Boston Way
Lanham, Maryland 20706

3 Henrietta Street
London WC2E 8LU England

Library of Congress Cataloging-in-Publication Data

Stebbins, Robert A.
Predicaments : moral difficulty in everyday life / Robert A. Stebbins.
p.   cm.
Includes bibliographical references and index.
1. Ethical problems.   2. Etiquette.   3. Interpersonal relations—
Moral and ethical aspects.   4. Social interaction.   I. Title.
BJ1031.S743   1993   302—dc20   93–2207 CIP

ISBN 0–8191–9212–0 (cloth : alk. paper)
ISBN 0–8191–9213–9 (pbk. : alk. paper)

To Christi

CONTENTS

ACKNOWLEDGEMENT

The permission to reprint the following articles written by the author is gratefully acknowledged:

Chapter 3: Putting people on: Deception of our fellowman in everyday life. *Social and Social Research* 59 (1975): 189-200.

Chapter 4: The social psychology of selfishness. *Canadian Review of Sociology and Anthropology* 18 (1981): 82-92.

Chapter 5: Situational ignorance and its consequences. *Humboldt Journal of Social Relations* 3 (1975): 13-18.

Chapter 6: Modesty, pride, and conceit. *Pacific Sociological Review* 15 (1972): 461-481

Chapter 7: Role distance, role distance behaviour and jazz musicians. *The British Journal of Sociology* 20 (1969): 406-415.

Chapter 8: The role of humour in teaching: Strategy and self-expression. In *Teacher strategies: Explorations in the sociology of the school*, edited by Peter Woods, 84-97. London, Eng.: Croom Helm, 1980.

INTRODUCTION

The sociology of everyday life has always held an immense fascination for me. It was probably just this fascination that predisposed me, during my graduate student days in the early 1960s, to read the books that Erving Goffman was writing at the time and study the related school of thought of symbolic interactionism. Goffman stood out among sociologists and anthropologists, including the symbolic interactionists, with his penchant for analyzing what one might call "everyday moral concepts," exemplified by a diversity of social interchanges such as insults, gaffes, embarrassment, selfishness, and put ons. They are the commonsense ideas shared and used by people in the community to describe, organize, and explain routine social occurrences whose rightness is problematic.

A scattered list of everyday moral processes has been unevenly explored over the years, chiefly as one-shot sorties of curiosity by sociologists who, as Goffman and I, found interest in one aspect or another of everyday life. Their's was a passing interest, however. So far as I know, the two of us remain alone in our continuing commitment to this area, for we have returned several times to study these so-called ordinary ideas. The initiative, however, was Goffman's; on could say he pioneered this kind of sociology. Here I am a follower, and my considerable indebtedness to him is expressed in citations throughout this book.

One vexing problem in the study of everyday moral concepts has been their apparent unrelatedness. The list in the first paragraph of this introduction illustrates the point. Sociologists have exacerbated the problem through their tendency to conduct "quick and dirty" studies of one such concept and then retreat, intellectual curiosity sufficiently satisfied, to the high ground of established research interests. Thus, due to a lack of systematic and enduring scientific attention, research on the everyday moral concept has languished at the qualitative-exploratory level of analysis. Here it has been further weakened by an absence of any significant theoretical elaboration that would come from developing overarching, or generic concepts I faced this problem when I made the decision to pull together the seven studies reported in this book. What do the moral concepts of deception (the put-on), selfishness, situational ignorance, conceit, role distance, humor, and aloneness have in common? Whereas there may be other strands of similarity, I found the idea of the predicament to be especially workable. Predicaments are the disagreeable interactive situations for which one participant there is particularly responsible and from which all participants who are affected by the first participant's actions can extricate themselves only with difficulty, if at all. They are important situated expressions of particular everyday moral concepts.

Predicaments are also fundamentally social and public, which distinguishes them from the much more personal and private form of predicament known as the dilemma. In the latter we must either choose between unsatisfactory alternatives forced on us by the convergence of circumstances beyond our control or deal with a difficult or persistent problem. Whether to divorce one's spouse or suffer on in a conflict-ridden union or pay the excessive rent for an apartment or the high payments for a housing mortgage exemplify the first form of dilemma. The second form is felt by many of the unemployed who try day in and day out to find work.

Moreover, the social predicament is itself an everyday moral concept, in this instance one that subsumes a considerable range of related concepts. As such, my interest, born over thirty years ago, continues. In the meantime the idea of the predicament, which is developed in chapter 1 and integrated into the framework of everyday life sociology in chapter 2, serves as one of the few generic concepts in the study of everyday moral ideas and, for that matter, in qualitative-exploratory research. This book, I believe, exemplifies both.

THE PREDICAMENT

Do you wish people to think well of you? Don't speak well of yourself (Blaise Pascal).

"I resent your remark," said the fifth grader. "And I'll give you just five seconds to take it back!"

"Oh, yeah," snarled the seventh grader. "Suppose I don't take it back in five seconds?"

"Well," said the first, "how much time do you want?"

"What do you mean," roared the politician, "by publicly insulting me in your old rag of a paper? I will not stand for it, and I demand an immediate apology."

"Just a moment," answered the editor. "Didn't the news appear exactly as you gave it to us, namely, that you had resigned as city treasurer?"

"It did, but where did you put it? - in the column under the heading 'Public Improvements.'"

There are times when life seems inescapably disagreeable. This sentiment prevails despite what we believe is our best effort at avoiding trouble, which we get into anyway because we have said or done something offensive to someone else. Fortunately most of the little scrapes we get into have few grave or long-term consequences. We deal with them on the spot, sometimes effectively, sometimes ineffectively, after which they pass and are for the most part forgotten. We may even vow we will never again let ourselves in for such trouble, although memories can be short and behavior, at times, less than completely controllable. So it may happen, as the years go by, that we wind up in similar disagreeable circumstances, thereby demonstrating anew the truth of George Santayana's sobering observation that "life is not a spectacle or a feast; it is a predicament."

Sociologists have yet to embrace the predicament as a formal area of research, which means some rudimentary conceptual work remains to be done. Let us make a start in this direction by developing a simple definition and three-dimensional classification: Predicaments refer to disagreeable interactive situations for which one participant there is particularly responsible and from which all participants who are affected by the first participant's actions can free themselves only with difficulty, if at all. Alternatively, participants are freed from the unsettling situation simply because it comes to an end in some way, rather than because they resolved its nastiness. In any case predicaments are important situated expressions of particular everyday moral concepts. What makes predicaments especially sociological is that they suck other people in the situation into the whirlpool of disagreeableness and indecision intentionally or unintentionally caused by an individual who has done or said something offensive to the others.

For want of a better word let us call the person who causes the predicament its *author*.[1] The direct cause of the predicament is the author's behavior in the immediate present, although such factors as the relevant attitudes, emotions, outlooks, and social statuses of all the participants, particularly those of the author, are related as background to the fateful act or acts triggering it. The solution to the predicament is anything but obvious, at least in part because no one who is party to it has, at the moment, sufficient freedom to maneuver within the situation or to leave it or sufficient ability to talk his or her way out of it.

If sociologists have failed to elevate the lowly predicament to the lofty status of a scientific concept, they have nevertheless studied the idea, albeit always under the names of related everyday moral concepts. To arrive at a preliminary understanding of what we mean by predicaments, let us briefly sample the scattered, sporadic literature on moral concepts. Although he never used these two terms in the technical sense being developed here, the study of moral concepts and their predicaments was once the special province of Erving Goffman (see, particularly, 1961; 1967). He defined and explored the nature and behavioral expressions of deference, demeanor, and embarrassment (see also Gross and Stone, 1964; Crozier, 1990). He went on to examine role distance (see also chapter 7 of this volume) and the commission of gaffes as well as the disagreeableness emerging from these distinctive situations.

That these concepts harbor the potential for predicaments is obvious except perhaps for the enactment of role distance. This term was coined by Goffman to identify the dislike (and its behavioral extension) of certain role expectations that, when carried out, threaten one's self-esteem. As chapter 7 demonstrates, it is the role distance behavior that can offend, leading in the course of events to a predicament.

Sociological analyses have been made of the everyday moral concepts of sarcasm (Ball, 1965; Seckman and Couch, 1989), insult (Flynn, 1977), gossip (Rosnow and Fine, 1976: chapter 6), jealous and envious behavior (Clanton and Smith, 1977; Davis, 1974), and breaches in the ways we are expected to address people (Sagarin, 1973; Gelles and Little, 1977). Similar discussions of the ways we account for or excuse our actions (e.g., Lyman and Scott, 1989: chapter 9) and disclaim responsibility for them (Hewitt and Stokes, 1975) show how these interactive strategies can sometimes be offensive and therefore a source of predicaments. Staring at others, when this offends, causes disagreeable encounters, at least for those others (e.g., Goffman, 1963: 16; Stebbins, 1976: 119-20). Georg Simmel's (1950: 330-34) analysis of secrecy demonstrates that, by concealing information wanted by others, the secretive person may provoke an unpleasant interaction. In a series of experiments Jones (1964: 165-66) found that some people react to ingratiation with embarrassment or even disgust, which transforms the setting into a predicament for them. Additionally, violations of privacy (e.g., Ashcraft and Scheflen, 1976: chapter 2; Schwartz, 1967) and trust (e.g., Griffin and Barnes, 1976) sometimes place all concerned in a predicament. The seven everyday moral concepts examined in the present book add to this literature. The predicaments associated with them come from putting people on, being selfish, ignoring of others' immediate interests (situational ignorance), talking conceitedly about self-achievement, taking role distance, using humor inappropriately, and seeking solitude, or aloneness.

There is a definite North Americanness about all this. It is not true, however, that Americans and Canadians have cornered the market on embarrassment, conceited talk, violations of trust, and the like. Rather, they have, as cultural observers, shown an exceptional interest among world sociologists in studying everyday moral concepts, a scholarly undertaking that is highly compatible with symbolic interactionism and its deep intellectual roots in American society.

Types of Predicaments

The broadest import of this book is found in its contribution to an eventual formal grounded theory of predicaments (Glaser and Strauss, 1967). The ideas in this chapter have been abstracted primarily from my own studies and secondarily from the studies of predicaments mentioned in the preceding section. So far as theoretical elaboration is concerned, what I have accomplished here is only a start; future studies of predicaments will add greatly to and modify, perhaps extensively, what is presented here.

Even casual observation leaves no doubt that predicaments are by no means all of a kind. At minimum, they can be classified by *duration* as short- or long-term, by *will* or *volition* as intended or unintended, and by *space* as direct or indirect interaction. To avoid overcomplicating this, the first exposition of the idea of predicament, let me simply indicate that any two or all three of the dimensions of duration, volition, and space can be combined to produce a number of valid subtypes (e.g., an intended, direct, short-term predicament).

Short-term predicaments, which include the predicaments and moral concepts listed earlier as well as those presented later in this book, are often conceived and resolved in one or a few situations. Long-term predicaments span considerably more time, possibly even several years, for instance, those occurring in interpersonal relationships that have grown increasingly bitter as they have evolved. Long-term predicaments are the product of accumulated short-term predicaments. The duration of a predicament is determined in part by how difficult it is to solve, with some longer-term predicaments being nearly unsolvable. Nonetheless the line separating the two types at this stage of conceptualization is intentionally if unavoidably vague for, lacking systematic scientific thought on the matter, there is need to avoid premature theoretical closure while we explore it further.

Sociological studies of long-term predicaments are more difficult to find than studies of their short-term counterparts. Two, however, are well-known, one of which is Max Scheler's (1961) description and elaboration of *ressentiment*, as he referred to it.[2] *Ressentiment* is the "repeated experiencing and reliving of a particular emotional response reaction against someone else" (Scheler, 1961: 39). Such experiencing arises from the accumulated repression of hatred, revenge, envy, and similar feelings. It grows and festers over a number of months, even years. Predicaments are generated when an author's actions turn another person's *ressentiment* inward as a repressed desire for revenge built on a hatred of and a wish to destroy the author (c.f., Denzin, 1984: 225).

The second example of a long-term predicament is provided by Edwin Lemert (1972: chapter 15) in his study of paranoia and its behavioral expressions. Paranoia, which is itself only a mental state, begins when an individual senses that others in his immediate social environment are "out to get" him or her in some significant way. When the individual communicates this outlook in later interaction with those others, they interpret his or her behavior as evidence of unjustified suspicion of their motives. This places them in a predicament, their distaste for which they communicate in various, and at times subtle, ways to the incipient paranoid, or author. The latter then reacts with suspicion to their changed behavior toward him or her. A vicious circle of short-term predicaments is thereby set in motion culminating in the mental state of paranoia and the social state of exclusion.

None of the studies of short- and long-term predicaments considered here uses the idea of predicament in the theoretical sense being developed in this chapter. They were all written from other perspectives. But it is clear that they, and possibly others still awaiting discovery, can be explained with the predicament frame of reference.

That predicaments may be either intended or unintended, indicates that some authors may not define them as predicaments at all. Nonetheless it is evident that those people in the interaction who are affected by them hold just such a definition. For example, if someone *wants* to embarrass, insult, or ingratiate another for the discomfort this can cause, then only the target of these acts can logically become embroiled in a predicament. To the extent the plan succeeds, its author basks happily in the other person's social agony. It is chiefly the unintended predicaments with which this book deals, however, since they appear to be the most common. They are also the most pathetic, inasmuch as the author inadvertently creates his or her own interpersonal misery.

The third type of predicament is based on spatial differences. In brief, predicaments can be experienced directly in face-to-face interaction or indirectly through information conveyed by a third party or by an impersonal vehicle. Whereas staring and situational ignorance are only possible in direct interaction with other people, most predicaments can be generated either directly or indirectly. We can ingratiate or be selfish in a letter or to someone's face. We can show resentment by refusing to attend a function or by talking to the resented person over coffee. The nature of my disclaimer for an act can reach the ears of the affected person be way of an intermediary or by way of a meeting at which I, as author, speak with the other person.

The Moral Basis of Predicaments

Offensive behavior provokes a predicament because it is judged by at least some of the other participants in the interaction to be wrong according to one or more rules. Goffman (1967: 51) explains how this judgment is made:

> In general then, when a rule of conduct is broken we find that two
> individuals run the risk of becoming discredited: one with an obligation,

> who should have governed himself by the rule; the other with an
> expectation, who should have been treated in a particular way because of
> this governance. Both actor and recipient are threatened.

> An act that is subject to a rule of conduct is, then, a communication, for
> it represents a way in which selves are confirmed - both the self for which
> the rule is an obligation and the self for which it is an expectation.

In other words the threat of being discredited is offensive; this threat, in
turn, gives rise to a predicament.

But there is more to it than this, for violating a rule of conduct is also
"wrong"; as such it is a moral question. Moreover the others may even see
the violation as intended (although it may not actually be intended), which
adds to its reprehensibility. Still the morality of predicaments is definitely
not one of high philosophical or ethical import, but only one of everyday
practicality with roots in the cultural terrain of etiquette. The rules violated
are the rules of etiquette, defined by Hockart (1931: 615) as the body of
forms of conventional decorum, or manners into which personal behavior
is cast. Etiquette refers to the principles of good breeding, or good taste as
respected by the larger community and to the rules we must follow during
official events as required by authority. In general we observe our rules of
etiquette when we avoid offending others with threats to discredit them,
when we avoid transgressing their moral expectations.

We should not lose sight of the fact that when it comes to predicaments
it takes at least two to tango: If the others remain unoffended, leave the
situation, or simply brush off the author's offensive behavior as insignificant, the predicament will be stillborn. For a full-blown predicament to
develop, the others must, as it were, somehow "make an issue" of the
violation of etiquette and, in this manner, create a general atmosphere of
unpleasantness that darkens the interaction.

Furthermore, in any predicament, the self-esteem of the participants
who are affected is invariably at stake. This too is a moral issue, as
Goffman so aptly communicated in the preceding quotation. Later in the
same article he added:

> It is therefore important to see that the self is in part a ceremonial thing,
> a sacred object which must be treated with proper ritual care and in turn
> must be presented in a proper light to others (Goffman, 1967: 91).

The author of the unintended predicament must confront the humiliating
implication, made apparent by the reactions of the others, that he or she has
inadvertently offended them. For the others, the author raises such self-
referent questions as: "how dare that individual treat me in this way," "who
does this person think I am to offend me like this." The others see

themselves as exploited, belittled, ignored, taken as naive, or similarly discredited by the author.

Predicaments and the everyday moral concepts from which they issue are an important sociological crossroad. In them the cultural world of morals and rules of etiquette meets the personal world of self-conception and the social world of situated human interaction. We could go on to identify a variety of background factors with which we might elaborate this brief statement yet, even in its present simplified form, it adequately communicates the essence of the idea of the predicament.

Predicaments for Whom?

No one escapes. Everyone is beset from time to time by predicaments, whatever the type, largely because they are unable to control all the forces bearing on their everyday lives. Nonetheless predicaments are not uniformly experienced throughout the community; for various reasons some people endure more of them than others. One set of reasons is demographic. Although the following chapters sometimes fail to demonstrate them as well as they might, some predicaments do seem to be correlated in special ways with particular demographic variables. To illustrate this association, let us consider several of these variables in connection with the predicaments mentioned earlier in this chapter.

Advancing age, partly because it is commonly accompanied by a growing level of sophistication about social life, is closely associated with certain predicaments. For instance, casual observation suggests that children typically stare more often, desire less privacy, and act more selfishly than adults. Moreover, when compared with younger adults, older adults have learned better how to avoid making gaffes. It is also likely that single people, including those who are divorced or widowed, crave less solitude than those who are married, especially when the latter have children at home.

Gender is another important demographic variable in the sociology of predicaments, but one about which there is still much to learn in this regard. The study reported in chapter 3 suggests that women put on men less often than the reverse, whereas this may turn out to be valid only for the sporting put-on as opposed to the discriminative and profitable types. Although no research has been conducted on the subject, women, to the extent that they are more or less constantly with their children, may seek aloneness and privacy more often than men.

Some intriguing questions remain to be explored in this area: Are men more inclined to behave conceitedly than women and women more inclined to behave modestly than men? Which of the two sexes is the more selfish, if either? Which is more likely to wisecrack or tell a joke? Do gender differences exist in the amount of jealousy and envy human beings feel or in the amount of staring they can tolerate?

Turning to ethnicity, we can only speculate (since the lack of data leaves no other choice) that recent immigrants to North America, especially those from Third World countries, will more often be authors of predicaments stemming from situational ignorance than earlier arrivals or native born people. Due to their relative ignorance of Western culture, they might also become the victims of put-ons more often. Although rarely studied at the interactive level as a predicament, there is ample evidence that certain immigrant groups foster resentment among those North Americans who believe the former have taken their jobs, residential space, political privilege, and symbols of group prestige (e.g., See and Wilson, 1988: 232-33). Cross-cultural differences may also affect the propensity to ingratiate others. Furthermore, ethnic groups and other minorities (e.g., women) may be especially vulnerable as targets of violations of trust and the ensuing predicaments. To the extent that they lack power, they must trust others to act as they claim they will (McCall and Simmons, 1978: 193).

What about the difference between rural and urban residence? Evidence from the study of the put-on suggests that the relative anonymity of the city is a fertile seedbed for this form of deception. Perhaps the violation of trust and the spiral of paranoid exclusion as described by Lemert are more likely to develop here as well. Finally, does the intimacy of rural life drive people to seek aloneness more often than the impersonality of the urban milieu?

As the final point in this discussion of the demographic correlates of predicaments, bear in mind that some of the latter may turn out, upon closer examination, to be actually or virtually unrelated to any of the former. At any rate I can think of no reason at this time why the predicaments born of gaffes, sarcasm, accounts, embarrassment, and disclaimers, should vary according to any demographic variable. Perhaps more thorough study of these forms will reveal a different relationship.

Predicaments Where?

Another reason why predicaments are unevenly experienced is that some are unevenly distributed among the social institutions of society. As with the demographic correlates of predicaments, considerably less information is available on the institutional correlates than is desirable. Still it is possible to generalize tentatively from the data that do exist.

The research reported in chapter 4 portraits selfishness as predominantly a family matter, although certainly not without example in the sphere of work as well. The predicaments that issue from staring and situational ignorance arise mostly in public places, especially those with commercial, recreational, and touristic functions. They are concentrated in our economic and leisure institutions. Since conceit revolves around talk about of self-achievement, we can conclude that the first is most prevalent in institutions where the second is valued, namely, work and serious leisure (i.e., amateur, hobbyist, and career volunteer pursuits, Stebbins, 1992).

Aloneness is chiefly a family, leisure, and religious strategy, for it can be realized here more often than at work where there is, in most cases, comparatively little opportunity for it. Put-ons, which thrive in impersonal settings, are nonetheless unequally distributed by type. The sporting variety tends to be limited to leisure and leisurelike settings, whereas the profitable and discriminative types, being more serious in import, are found mostly at work (both deviant and nondeviant) and in politics.

As with some of the demographic variables, predicaments emerge that appear to have no institutional boundaries. The demeaning role expectations that provoke role distance are found almost everywhere in life (including education) as are the situations that generate humor. Likewise, gaffes, jealousy, secrecy, embarrassment, resentment, sarcasm, ingratiation, violations of trust and privacy, and the use of accounts and disclaimers seem to exist throughout North American society. Lemert (1972: 252) discussed the wide variety of institutional settings where the exclusion that engenders paranoia is likely to take root.

Short-Term Predicaments

The selection of everyday moral concepts and predicaments published here is only a partial, rather unrepresentative sample of the range of possible short-term predicaments a typical American or Canadian is likely to face in the course of his or her routine activities. Still these seven predicaments illustrate the broader problem everyone faces from time to time: How to manage unexpected disagreeableness originating in the behavior of others and, sometimes, in ourselves.

This book looks at some of our moral concepts and predicaments and some of the ways to avoid the latter or, where they are unavoidable, at some of the ways to solve them. Chapters 3, 4, and 5 devote more attention to the predicaments themselves than to what we typically do about them. In the main these chapters describe, as sources of distinct moral difficulty in social life, how people put each other on, behave selfishly, and show their situational ignorance. Chapter 6, which is on modesty, pride, and conceit, is a transitional statement: It not only describes the predicament caused by conceited talk about self-achievement, it also suggests how it can be prevented by speaking modestly or proudly. Chapters 7, 8, and 9 concentrate on the strategic uses of role distance, humor, and aloneness, although each is also described in considerable detail. All three can be enacted in ways offensive to other people in the situation, the outcome of which is a predicament. Chapters 8 and 9, in particular, address the question of how to avoid short-term predicaments. The use of humor and solitude for this purpose is extremely broad, reaching into nearly every corner of everyday life.

The Limits of Predicaments

The very disagreeableness of predicaments is enough to motivate most people to try to avoid them as often as possible. Everyone manages to do this in at least some of their relations with others, suggesting that the avoidance of predicaments is a conscious act even if causing them is sometimes not. Yet, to repeat an earlier observation, we are not always entirely in control of our own behavior (hence gaffes and staring, for instance) nor are we always able to predict how people will interpret and react to the ways in which we do mean to behave. Therefore as unpleasant as it often is and as much as we would like to avoid it, Santayana was right: "life is . . . a predicament." He was, by the way, an American writer and philosopher who observed the same cultural and behavioral landscape as we have been observing throughout this chapter and will continue to observe throughout this book.

Fortunately for us all, the predicaments that we fail to avoid and must suffer through do have an end. Some of these - they usually involve strangers - end with no important consequences, as seen in some episodes of situational ignorance (e.g., people who talk loudly in a cinema or drive slowly during rush hour). They occur, annoy us, come to an end, and perhaps even leave a residue of irritation for a few minutes or even a few hours, but are generally soon forgotten in the swirl of more important interests and preoccupations. The conceited talk and role distance behavior of people in certain social settings can have a similar impact.

Among the inconsequential predicaments are those where the author apologizes for his or her moral transgression. The apology assuages the offense to the point where its consequences are blunted. Strange as it may seem, it is the offended person or persons who, as it were, must close the deal by accepting the apology proffered by the author.

> This power [accepting the apology] entails a profound moral obligation since the helpless offender, *in consideration for nothing more than a speech*, asks for nothing less than the conversion of righteous indignation and betrayal into unconditional forgiveness and reunion (Tavuchis, 1991: 35).

And what if the proffered apology is rejected?

This is the point where predicaments can become more problematic. One, they can lead to attempts at revenge, a process well exemplified in the chapters on selfishness and the put-on. It is also likely that insults trigger the desire for revenge. Two, predicaments springing from such moral concepts as selfishness and the insult may lead others in the situation to avoid the author from thereon. Three, when people are trapped in a relationship with someone, they may have endure a long-term predicament of a certain kind for many months, perhaps many years. They may have to put up with the recurrent insults from or embarrassing acts of a superior, the secrecy or jealousy of equals, or the ingratiation of underlings.

However we perpetrate, experience, and handle the predicaments we either create or become involved in, it is important to remember that they are far from being isolated events either for ourselves or, often, for the larger social world in which we operate. The sociology of everyday life, of which the study of predicaments is but one important part, has now advanced to the point where it constitutes a theoretical framework broad enough to show how these scrapes with others fit the larger social picture. The structures and processes of this framework provide the social backdrop for the stage on which our moral concepts and their predicaments play.

Endnotes

1.   The English language lacks a precise word to describe the idea of author as defined here. The standard meaning of author suggests that certain consequences are intended to follow from the author's actions, whereas the author of a predicament does not necessarily intend to cause it.

2.   As Denzin (1984: 225) observes, Scheler's *ressentiment* is not equivalent to the English word "resentment." Nor was there an equivalent in German at the time that Scheler wrote. Yet, his definition of *ressentiment*,

which was the same as in French, is now regarded as old (c.f., *Le Petit Robert 1*). The modern definition of *ressentiment* is translatable into English as resentment, where the English word has its etymological roots in its modern French counterpart.

References

Ashcraft, Norman, and Albert E. Scheflen
　　1976　*People space.* Garden City, N.Y.: Anchor Books.

Ball, Donald W
　　1965　Sarcasm as sociation: The rhetoric of interaction. *Canadian Review of Sociology and Anthropology* 2:190-98.

Clanton, Gordon, and Lynn G. Smith
　　1977　*Jealousy.* Englewood Cliffs, N.J.: Prentice-Hall.

Crozier, W. Ray (ed.)
　　1990　*Shyness and embarrassment: Perspective from social psychology.* Cambridge, Eng.: Cambridge Univeristy Press.

Davis, Kingsley
　　1974　Jealousy and sexual property. In *Sociology for pleasure*, edited by Marcello Truzzi, 141-52. Englewood Cliffs, N.J.: Prentice-Hall.

Denzin, Norman K.
　　1984　*On understanding emotion.* San Francisco, Calif.: Jossey-Bass.

Flynn, Charles P.
　　1977　*Insult and society.* Port Washington, N,Y.: Kennikat Press.

Gelles, Richard J., and Craig B. Little. Form of address: Yardstick and stumbling block of social interaction. In *Our sociological eye*, edited Arthur B. Shostak. Port Washington, N.Y.: Alfred.

Glaser, Barney G., and Anselm L. Strauss
　　1967　*The discovery of grounded theory.* Chicago: Aldine.

Goffman, Erving
　　1961　*Encounters.* Indianapolis, Ind.: Bobbs-Merrill.

Goffman, Erving.
1963 *Stigma*. Englewood Cliffs, N.J.: Prentice-Hall.

Goffman, Erving
1967 *Interaction ritual*. Chicago: Aldine.

Griffin, Kim, and Richard Barnes
1976 *Trust of self and others*. Columbus, Ohio: Merrill.

Gross, Edward, and Gregory P. Stone
1964 Embarrassment and the analysis of role requirements. *American Journal of Sociology* 70: 1-15.

Hewitt, John P., and Randall Stokes
1975 Disclaimers. *American Sociological Review* 40: 1-11.

Hockart, A.M.
1931 Etiquette. In *Encyclopedia of the social sciences*, vol. 5, edited by Edwin R.A. Seligman and Alvin Johnson, 615-17. New York: Macmillan.

Jones, Edward E.
1964 *Ingratiation*. New York: Appleton-Century-Crofts.

Lemert, Edwin
1972 *Human deviance, social problems, and social control*, 2nd ed. Englewood Cliffs, N.J.: Prentice-Hall.

Lyman, Stanford, and Marvin B. Scott
1989 *A sociology of the absurd*, 2nd ed. Dix Hills, N.J.: General Hall.

McCall, George J., and J.L. Simmons
1978 *Identities and interactions*, rev. ed. New York: Free Press.

Rosnow, Ralph L., and Gary Alan Fine
1976 *Rumor and gossip*. New York: Elsevier.

Sagarin, Edward
1973 Etiquette, embarrassment, and forms of address. In *People in places: The Sociology of the familiar edited by Arnold Birenbaum and Edward Sagarin*. New York: Praeger.

Schwartz, Barry
    1967   The social psychology of privacy. *American Journal of Sociology* 73: 741-52.

Seckman, Mark A., and Carl J. Couch
    1989   Jocularity, sarcasm, and relationships: An empirical study. *Journal of Contemporary Ethnography* 18:327-44.

See, Katherine O., and William J. Wilson
    1988   Race and ethnicity. In *Handbook of sociology*, edited by Neil J. Smelser, 223-42. Newbury Park, Calif.: Sage.

Simmel, Georg
    1950   *The sociology of Georg Simmel*, translated by Kurt Wolff. New York: Free Press.

Stebbins, Robert A.
    1976   *Commitment to deviance*. Westport, Conn.: Greenwood.

Stebbins, Robert A.
    1992   *Amateurs, professionals, and serious leisure*. Montreal and Kingston: McGill-Queen's University Press.

Tavuchis, Nicholas
    1991   *Mea culpa: A sociology of apology and reconciliation*. Stanford, Calif.: Stanford University Press.

Chapter 2

EVERYDAY LIFE SOCIOLOGY

Have you found your life distasteful?
My life did and does smack sweet.
Was your youth of pleasure wasteful?
Mine I saved and hold complete.
Do your joys with age diminish?
When mine fail me, I'll complain.
Must in death your daylight finish?
My sun sets to rise again

(Robert Browning)

We saw in chapter 1 how predicaments and their related moral concepts form a major sociological crossroad, where the cultural world of morals and etiquette meets the personal world of self-conception and the social world of situated interactions. This theoretical junction is located at the center of a vast theoretical territory referred to in recent years with increasing frequency as the sociology of everyday life. Several fields examine the social aspects of everyday life, most notably dramaturgy, phenomenology, ethnomethodology, labeling theory, existential sociology, and symbolic interactionism. Patricia Adler and her colleagues (1987: 218) believe these fields now constitute an identifiable body of theory concerned with a set of common empirical problems.

What are these problems? Maffesoli (1989: v) describes everyday life sociology as the study of "lived experience . . . of feelings, passions, images, and differences." By framing the rudimentary statement of predicaments and moral concepts in the larger theoretical context of everyday life sociology, we enrich considerably our understanding of these two closely related ideas. This is done in general terms here and in specific terms in next seven chapters, where each chapter treats a particular predicament and moral concept in detail.

There is no need to undertake a compehensive review and synthesis in this chapter of the sprawling literature on the sociology of everyday life; this has already been carried out by Adler, Adler, and Fontana (1987). Instead, I will extract and interrelate several main ideas from the literature, ideas related to many or all of the predicaments discussed later. Two advantages flow from such an approach: The central notions of predicament and moral concept will be anchored in broader sociological theory and the theory will receive additional empirical grounding from the studies reported in this book.

Predicaments and Everyday Life

The study of predicaments and moral concepts can be conducted on one or more of the three general levels of analysis and theory of the sociology of everyday life: personal, interactive, and sociocultural. On whichever level or levels a researcher decides to work, it is necessary, if he or she is to contribute to this branch of sociology, to study people in their natural settings as they experience their daily, routine existence. This, as Adler, Adler, and Fontana (1987: 219) put it, is "the most fundamental and central emphasis of everyday life sociology." The predicaments examined in the next seven chapters were, wherever possible, explored from a naturalist perspective.

Personal Level

At the center of every individual's personal existence lies his or her ego, or *self*, defined by Lindesmith, Strauss, and Denzin (1991: 7) as "all that persons call their own at a particular moment." The self - the very core of personality - consists of two sides: the active, spontaneous, mostly unconscious side and the socially generated, largely knowable side. The social side, which is often referred to as the "self-concept," holds the greater interest for most sociologists, particularly the symbolic interactionists. Here, based on socially established criteria, individuals appraise and give meaning to their selves and then, when appropriate, communicate these appraisals to others. The appraisals and their communication are eminently social processes, inasmuch as they are carried out in interactive situations, in the company of other people.

The acts leading to a predicament often have a profound effect on the self-concepts of both the author and the others. This happens when the behavior of the former offends and discredits the latter, calling into question their self-worth at the moment. This effect also gives substance to the observation made in the preceding chapter that the self is a sacred object, an entity to be treated with utmost care.

Predicaments can also tarnish one's image in the social "looking glass" (Cooley, 1902), the reflected assessments of oneself communicated through the actions of others in the situation. People caught in a predicament typically see themselves in the mirror provided by the author's behavior as exploited, belittled, ignored, taken as naive, and the like. Such a reflection, however, apparently leads to few enduring changes in the self-appraisals of the others in the predicament, for they did not create it; their reactions were externally caused (Felson, 1992: 1745). Enduring change could nevertheless take place in the self-concept of an author who unintentionally brought on a predicament.

Felson (1992: 1747) goes on to note that, although human behavior is habitual and automatic much of the time, awareness of self is especially acute when, among other conditions, disruptions occur in the social interaction. Predicaments are disruptive by their very nature; therefore they are a source of momentary and in this instance unpleasant self-consciousness among those whom they affect. The delicateness of a person's self-concept and hence the strong likelihood of finding it at the center of a predicament are evident in the following exchange between a female coal miner and a male coworker:

> If the men know you're going to embarrass them if they push you too far, they have more respect for you. . . . We were picking some coal and the stuff flies all over and you got to pull your shirt out and get the coal out. And this one guy said, "I got something for you." . . . He was being provocative about it, reaching into his pants and throwing coal at me. Finally, I said, "[Male co-worker], if it takes you that long to find it, then I don't want it." And the whole crew just cracked up and he got real embarrassed. He got kidded about that for a long time (Yount, 1991: 414).

Biography

According to Weigert (1983: 4) a biography is "an interpretive reconstruction of the meanings of a person's selected experiences"; it is often presented as a story, usually a life story. Personal biographies are related to predicaments and the sociology of everyday life in at least two ways. First, whether people in a predicament are offended by the actions of the author partly depends on how each person's biography has evolved to that point in time. The section in Chapter 1 about the categories of people who experience different predicaments bears to some extent on this assertion. Of more direct import, however, is the observation that certain statuses, accomplishments, experiences, and relationships in our past predispose us to interpret in special ways the actions of the author in the present. Depending on the interpretation, a predicament may develop.

For example, from interviewing a sample of exoffenders, most of whom lived in towns or small cities, I discovered how upset they became when someone stared at them (Stebbins, 1976: 119-120). Several respondents described how they became objects from time to time of a demeaning curiosity, in their case an unseemly fascination with the real-life appearance of a thief and former prisoner. Some of them reported confronting the starers about the inappropriateness of their actions and, in so doing, creating predicaments for the latter.

Lemert's (1972) study of the social conditions leading to paranoia contains an excellent illustration of the way unfavorable past experiences with a paranoid person can influence interpetations of his or her present behavior as in some way intolerable (e.g., insulting, aggressive, arrogant, exploitative). The behavior and interpretations eventually become the *raison d'étre* for excluding the hapless individual from certain important activities which, in turn, he or she treats as evidence that "they are out to get me." Soon a long-term predicament develops, as manifested in a series of offensive incidents involving the paranoid and those with whom he or she routinely associates.

Second, biographies can also influence the behavior of authors and would-be authors. For instance, they may have learned earlier in life how certain actions create predicaments for themselves and other people around them. Whether they want to create or avoid these predicaments, their past experiences now help them foresee the reactions of others to their present behavior. Flynn (1977: 92) provides an appropriate example in his summary of research on the way insults are used in various societies to socialize young men into the values and traits of fighting and military prowess. By improving themselves in the arts of combat and defense, some men, he concluded, learn to avoid insults to their fighting ability and consequently the predicaments the insults can engender.

Role-Identities

McCall and Simmons (1978: 65) define role-identity as an individual's "imaginative view of himself as he likes to think of himself being and acting as an occupant of a particular social position or status." Role-identities are a major component of a person's self-concept. They also serve as vehicles by which he or she can consider future projections of the self through identity related personal goals. Although I know of no examples in the literature on the sociology of everyday life, it is easy to imagine how a predicament could emerge because an author did or said something to discredit someone else's highly valued goals and related role-identities.

To illustrate this point, let me recount a personal experience. While doing research several years ago for a book on deviant behavior, I interviewed a male transsexual who wanted to become a woman to learn more about the life-style of transsexuals in general. Midway through the interview we went for refreshments at a nearby snack bar where, as the two of us approached the cashier, I said I would pay for *his* coffee. This was a most unfortunate gaffe, for my respondent was dressed, made up, and named as a woman, all in anticipation of surgical changes soon to be made. Although the cashier showed no sign of recognizing the discrepancy in identity I had just inadvertently fostered, Danielle was both angered and embarrassed by my blunder. The resulting predicament sprang from the way I publicly discredited the cherished future role-identity of female by treating him (her) in the present as a male.

Interactional Level

Self, self-concept, biography, and role-identity are expressed in interaction with other people in the nearly countless social situations through which we pass in everyday life. Since these entities and processes are so intimately tied to our exchanges with those others, it is impossible in the final analysis to truly separate the personal and interactive levels. The complexity of the matter is seen in the processes by which the people around us judge our personalities and our actions, give us standards for comparison, help us realize personal and collective goals and, when it comes to predicaments, create offensive interactions or suffer through the ones we create. Thus the separation of the two levels in this chapter is more analytic than real. It is done to show that the concepts of self, self-concept, biography, and role-identity are theoretically closer to personality than to the interactive processes considered in this section: definition of the situation, impression management, emotionality, and negotiation.

The following definition of the *definition of the situation* is a distillate of several different definitions of this idea coined over the years in symbolic interactionism and related fields:

> The definition of the situation is the overall meaning of the immediate situation for each individual participating in it. It is established through conscious interpretation and synthesis of its relevant personal, social, physical, and temporal considerations and through its relevant preformed

cultural structures that each individual internalizes and carries from situation to situation (taken with modification from Stebbins, 1986: 134).

The definition of the situation is a major theoretical linchpin. It links the cultural and structural contexts within which a person operates to his or her goals in the immediate setting as these are realized through interaction with other people within particular periods of time in particular physical locations.

In addition, everyday life can be described as a continuous flow of situations to be entered and defined, continuity there being realized in the ways we construct and reconstruct our biographies. Moreover, similar definitions of the same type of situation by many different people may crystallize into new social or cultural structures or changes in existing ones. The new formations, in turn, become part of the social context within which we define future situations of this sort.

The predicaments described and analyzed in the subsequent chapters rely heavily on the concept of the definition of the situation for two reasons. The primary reason is that, when the author and others nearby define a situation as a predicament, they endow it with special meanings. True, whereas the events of the moment are understandable in everyday life terms, they are nonetheless highly significant because they hold unfavorable consequences for the self-concept and role-identities of each individual. The secondary, and more personal, reason stems from my long-standing interest in the definition of the situation; after studying the idea for more than twenty-five years, I cannot help looking for its expression in every walk of life.

The foregoing definition of the definition of the situation was elaborated from research and theory on the subject carried out in ethogeny, ethnomethodology, and symbolic interactionism (Stebbins, 1986). According to this synthesis, one of the most significant contributions made by the first two fields is the proposition, expressed here in Rom Harré's (1977) words, that "we carry around preformed structures or templates leading to situated behavioral or product structures." The concept of preformed structures closely resembles Goffman's (1974) concept of "frame," or the set of social rules and categories (of people, things, events, conditions) that individuals learn during socialization and call up as presuppositions when they define situations. These rules and categories are part of our cultural heritage and, although scientifically knowable, the typical actor is rarely aware of them in everyday life. In other words they are assumed.

George Gonos (1977) observed that, on the one hand, symbolic interactionists working in this area have been chiefly concerned with various types of situations and their meanings, meanings with which acculturated people are typically quite familiar. On the other hand, the interactionists have tended to ignore the cultural antecedents these same people bring to a given situation and with which acculturated people typically have little familiarity. These antecedents subtly shape every person's definition of that situation.

The violation of an everyday moral principle calls up in all concerned a special frame of preformed meanings and associated rules. That is, every moral frame provides a standard by which we can judge an action (define the situation) as offensive and therefore as wrong. This generalized standard must still be applied to actual situations, however; it must be adapted to the culture of the local group or setting. The frame, its moral standard, and its accompanying rules constitute what Freilich (1991) calls the "proper file," which must inevitably be adapted situationally through the "smart file" of local culture. Both files may even contain certain rules for managing ensuing predicaments, although they are missing from the following description of the frame of sarcasm:

> Sarcasm is, of course, a common everyday linguistic form of biting communication, especially, it would seem, an oral one, with its locus in intimate settings. . . . Most generally, it is probably true that sarcasm requires not only a set of appropriate words, sharply and uniquely relevant to the particular situation, but also a presentational context which allows the use of such arts of communication as inflection and intonation, gesture, timing, and facial and postural expression.

Ordinarily it is not enough that the proper potentially sarcastic words and phrases be presented; they must also be accompanied by ancillary elements of communication which summon up a sarcastic totality, that is, by the over- and under-emphasis of key symbols involving not only words, but also tone and expression (Ball, 1965: 191-192). Rules for managing sarcastic predicaments could be discovered in an ethnographic study designed for this purpose, but such a project is yet to be undertaken.

Impression Management

Effectively enacted sarcasm requires a good deal of impression management, or the "attempt by one person . . . to affect the perceptions of her or him by another person . . . " (Schneider, 1981: 25). Impression management is a conceptual stock-in-trade in the interdisciplinary field of dramaturgy. Here most social scientists work from the assumption that human social behavior has important expressive consequences (Brissett and Edgley, 1990: 6).

One problem facing a person embroiled in the unpleasant business of a predicament is how to select an appropriate public front as he or she reacts to it. Harrington (1992) found, for instance, that people attempt to deny their embarrassment both by downplaying the upsetting event and by laughing it off. It is likewise for those subjected to ingratiation:

> The important common feature of the vast majority of reactions to positive gestures from others is the communication of appreciation for their benevolent intentions. What may be crassly instrumental flattery is thus publicly interpreted as well- intentioned or normative flattery if it is not accepted as a matter of course. . . . Regardless of what he really thinks of . . .[the author's] intentions, . . . [the other person] is to an important extent bound by the face-work contract to avoid taking umbrage at . . . [the author's] overtures (Jones, 1964: 162-163).

Goffman (1967) stressed the importance of examining "face work" wherever people manage their impressions, an analytic approach that we may also apply to the management of impressions during predicaments.

Emotionality

The relatively new speciality of the sociology of emotions holds great promise for the study of offensive behavior. Those who study emotion from a sociological perspective treat human behavior as motivated by both rationality and irrationality - a particularly apt assumption when it comes to people's reactions to predicaments. Peggy Thoits (1989: 318) identified four universal components in the sociological definitions of emotion she examined:

> Emotions involve: (a) appraisals of a situational stimulus or context, (b) changes in physiological or bodily sensations, (c) the free or inhibited display of expressive gestures, and (d) a cultural label applied to specific constellations of one or more of the first three components.

All four components need not be present at once to experience an emotion or recognize the expression of one in someone else's behavior.

In harmony with this condition, many sociologists concentrate on one or two component only. Some stress the biological underpinnings of emotions (e.g., Mazur, 1985; Rossi, 1984), whereas others minimize or even ignore this component. Franks (1985) and Hochschild (1983), for instance, argue that emotions call out, moderate, and shape feelings in situations. They examine the ways in which emotions get labelled and assessed by those who are present in the interaction and how this may force the emotive person to manage his or her mental state in particular ways. Emotions are also interpreted with reference to the cultural frames and structural conditions related to the situation in question. Correspondingly, certain emotional expressions are expected in certain situations, as in funerals and weddings, or automatically present, as in accidents or life-threatening attacks.

Denzin (1984: 66) says that, because it is inevitably related to specific situations and contexts, an emotion locates people in time and space. Moreover the emotion may generalize, becoming a routine aspect of everyday life and acquiring a place in our personal biography and the social world in which we live. But emotion always takes the individual's self as its reference point; in Denzin's words "emotion is self-feeling."

Predicaments offer an excellent laboratory for the study of certain emotions. These emotions, given the offensive nature of predicaments, are always negative: for example, fear (in paranoid encounters), anger (in insults and staring), shame (in embarrassment), and hate (in deference). Anger was especially evident in the predicaments intentionally created by the experimenters in Wolff's (1973: 40) study of pedestrian behavior on New York sidewalks:

> When the experimenters did not cooperate in the step-and-slide [an evasion maneuver] and bumping ensued, in addition to the pedestrians' turning around and staring, remarks were sometimes made: "Whatsa madda" "Ya blind?" "Whyn't ya look whea ya goin?" Ya crazy?"

These predicaments were the result of feigned situational ignorance. As part of the etiquette of urban street life we expect approaching pedestrians to cooperatively steer a course of noncontact as they pass. Violation of this expectation, especially when no extenuating circumstances are apparent (e.g., being blind, carrying a bulky package), provokes anger at the presumed heedlessness of the uncooperative individual on the sidewalk.

Negotiation

The remaining facet of everyday life to consider at the interactive level is the process of negotiation. It is based on a pervasive relationship in social interaction that has gone unmentioned to this point in this chapter, namely, power, or the ability to control the behavior of others in a social situation and thereby dominate them. With reference to predicaments it is the combination of power and situational negotiation that interests us, as opposed to what we might call "organizational" negotiation, which is found, for example, in labor relations or international affairs. Situational negotiation is essentially "bargaining or haggling over the terms of exchange of social rewards. . . . It takes the form of an argument or debate over who each person is" (McCall and Simmons, 1978: 137-138). Bargaining is necessary because no one in the situation has the power to assert with finality his or her own will. Negotiation is an overreaching process composed of several subprocesses, including compromising, reaching tacit agreements, and making deals (Strauss, 1978: 1). Of primary importance in the study of predicaments is the situational negotiation over the issues of social identity, interactive roles, and personal agendas.

According to McCall and Simmons, we occasionally wind up in situations where one or more people there feel they must negotiate an important social identity. When this happens, those who are present reach either an agreement or a compromise about the status of each person. In the negotiation of interactive roles, the focus shifts to the behavior allowed in the setting. Agendas must also be negotiated; they are the schedules of activities a person hopes to carry out over a period of time such as a day, week, or month. We negotiate these with others who also have an interest in the way we spend the time in question.

Who negotiates what with whom depends on the power of each person in the negotiation, which depends, in turn, on the nature and extent of each person's resources and his or her ability to mobilize them. Hall (1987: 14) defines a resource as "any attribute, possession, or circumstance that . . . [negotiators] may use to achieve ends." The power resources exchanged in negotiations are nearly infinite; they include strength, skill, weapons, money, honor, knowledge, authority, equipment, and sexual favors. These resources are unevenly distributed in society. Moreover, in some situations usually powerful people may be unable to mobilize the resources they possesses and need at that moment. At that moment, then, they have less power than they normally have in such circumstances.

Predicaments appear to be by-products of situational negotiations, albeit not always insignificant by-products. While negotiating an identity, interactive role, or agenda, negotiating individuals may behave selfishly, secretively, or insultingly. Or they may breach the norms of deference, privacy, or some other form of etiquette. Perhaps one person in the situation lies or mistakes the identity or intentions of another. We can speculate that the more intense the negotiation the more likely a predicament of some sort will develop, for those involved are more likely to lose emotional control and somehow offend the others. Alternatively, they may intentionally offend them in their desperation to get the best of the bargain.

Insult and negotiation mingle in the following episode reported by Sugrue (1982: 287-289), where a physician attempts to define as mentally disordered a recalcitrant female patient who has developed an intense dislike for the hospital in which she is staying and the medical procedures being used to cure her bleeding ulcer. The imputation of mental disorder is insulting, which leads her to try to negotiate this identity with her doctor:

(D = Doctor; P = Patient)

(There is a knock at the door)

P: If it's a doctor don't come in.

D: Hi - how do you feel today? You look much better.

P: Since I look so damn good and feel ok, get rid of this tubing and let me go home.

D: Don't be so irrational, if I let you go home you'd be back in 24 hours in serious condition.

P: Don't be dramatic - just let me out of this place. I hate it here.

D: Pretend it's the Hilton and relax.

P: For what it cost I could be Europe and really relax and besides that I don't live on Fantasy Island. I can't pretend it's the Hilton when it feels like a prison.

D: Well, your tests look better.

P: I don't care. I want to go home today or else I want to die. I hate being locked up.

D: Stop crying and grow up.

P: Easy for you to say, you come and go as you please. You ain't stuck here.

D: I'm not a pediatrician, stop crying.

P: I'll cry whenever I want. I hate this place and I want out. . . .

D: You've been acting depressed and the nurses mentioned your behaviors - it's obvious that you are not oriented to long hospital stays. You need some anti- depressants and I'll send a psychiatrist in to talk to you.

P: Kiss my ass. I want no drugs, no shrink and I think that it's pretty fucking healthy I'm not oriented to long hospital stays - have the stupid nurses told you or charted their negligence, no of course not, it's the patient's fault.

D: You obviously cannot be reasoned with at this time.

P: Get the fuck out of my room. Take your goddam charts, tests and other crap with you. You act like God. . . .

D: Don't say things you don't mean. The anti-depressants will make you feel better. . . .

P: No way!!!

D: Are you afraid?

P: I'm not crazy so I need no drugs and no shrink. . . .

D: The drugs will give you a better perspective.

P: Fuck you - no drugs. What did you make a misdiagnosis? So you screw up and then give me drugs for being crazy so you can dismiss my complaints and cover your own ass. . . .

D: A psychiatrist will help you see things as they are.

P: No shrink. . . .

D: Look, you cannot discuss things now. You are in no shape to make decisions. Let the psychiatrist help you.

P: Drop dead. Mention that I'm crazy again and I'll sue you. . .

D: Calm down and we'll talk later.

P: There's nothing to talk about. Now get out of here and shut up.

Shortly after this exchange, a nurse came to the patient's room to ask if she would like to take a tranquilizer or see a psychiatrist. Both were refused again. All in all, the predicament appeared to end, as many predicaments do, unresolved. Although the patient was insulted at being labeled mentally disordered, she did successfully negotiate two aspects of this imputation: she neither swallowed the antidepressants nor saw a psychiatrist. She failed, however, to negotiate her release from the hospital. The label of mentally disordered was applied but, owing to negotiation, it failed to stick.

The heated exchange between the patient and her physician nicely illustrates the situational type of negotiation considered in this section. As is true for other forms of interaction, such negotiation can serve as the foundation for more enduring sociocultural phenomena.

Sociocultural Level

As Anselm Strauss (1978) has observed, situational negotiation can lead to something more profound than the mere settlement of a problem in which no one present has the power to fully realize his or her aims. A set of negotiations can become the basis for a new or reconstituted social order, for new social arrangements or new patterns of relations among the people involved in or affected by the negotiation. This is social change which, according to the sociologically inclined phenomenologists, is "reflexive"; the changes become the context for later negotiation. The phenomenologists join the symbolic interactionists in viewing human action as the ultimate starting point for the creation, maintenance, and change of all culture and social structure, however suprahuman and abstract the latter two sometimes become. In addition human-made culture and structure guide social interaction by means of the society's relevant cultural frames. This sequence is circular, or dialectic and logically consistent with Strauss's observation that all social orders are negotiated to some extent.

One criticism of Strauss's ideas on the negotiated order concentrates on their lack of adequate articulation with the general theories of sociology as well as with the more abstract social structures in society (Stryker, 1990: 19-20). A conceptual gap exists between the everyday life process of negotiation in situations and such all-encompassing entities as society, community, social class, and large-scale organization. David Maines (1982) coined the term "mesostructure" to help bridge this gap.

Mesostructure refers to the intermediate level of interaction between immediate social interaction (where situational negotiation takes place) and the abstract levels of society, community, and similar entities. At the mesostructural level human interaction is still discernible, as seen, for example, in the formation and operation of social networks (e.g., Fine and Kleinman, 1983) and small groups and the accomplishment of collective activity (Hall, 1987: 12-13). Collective activity is a coordinated sequence of social acts carried out by two or more persons in relation to certain goals or social objects. In addition, the typical urban community is organized along the lines of its many social worlds, which constitutes yet another side of mesostructure. According to Unruh (1979: 115)

> a *social world* must be seen as a unit of social organization which is diffuse and amorphous in character. Generally larger than groups or organizations, social worlds are not necessarily defined by formal boundaries, membership lists, or spatial territory. . . . A social world must be seen as an internally recognizable constellation of actors, organizations, events, and practices which have coalesced into a perceived sphere of interest and involvement for participants. Characteristically, a social world lacks a powerful centralized authority structure and is delimited by . . . effective communication and not territory nor formal group membership (Unruh, 1979:115).

The urban community abounds with social worlds that have formed around occupations, sports, hobbies, volunteer activities, the fine and popular arts, and other substantial interests.

Maines went on to discuss time as a significant dimension in the analysis of mesostructures. Change is omnipresent and always juxtaposed with permanence, both of which owe their existence to human action and both of which take time to effect. The time dimension forces us to consider the past, present, and future as well as their interrelationship. Of utmost importance for the study of predicaments is the idea that pasts enforce limits and constraints, since they can never be undone, only reinterpreted (Hall, 1987: 15). What happened in the past or is happening in the present may lead us to predict what will happen in the future. And what we expect to happen in the future may condition our behavior in the present.

Superimposed on these more or less natural segments of time are the many artificial, or arbitrary temporal arrangements of the community. They include the standard lengths of time allotted for various activities; the times at which they typically start and end; their place in our daily, weekly, monthly, or yearly calendars. Present and future structures of this sort can sometimes be negotiated or renegotiated according to the interests and power of those concerned.

Margaret Mead, in writing about jealousy in the primitive society of Dobu near New Guinea, picturesquely describes how the predicaments it causes can alter the local mesostructure:

> A man who has been discovered as the seducer of another man's wife, is liable to have a spear thrust in his back. But against his wife's intrigue with one of her village "brothers" a man has no such redress. If he protests, his wife's relatives simply throw him out of the village. Should he slay a member of his wife's village, it would become a "place of blood" to him and he might never enter it again. In desperate case indeed is the man whose wife has betrayed him with a village "brother" and in such case also is the wife of the latter who also is only an in-law and a stranger in the village. In such cases the betrayed spouse has only one resource, a sort of pseudo-suicide in which fish poison, which may or may not be fatal, is taken. The kin of the unfaithful spouse, alarmed lest death will follow which will involve them in a blood feud, may then exercise pressure and reunite the pair. But marriages maintained by attempted suicides against odds such as these, do not make for security and happiness, but rather for suspicion and jealousy (Mead, 1977: 122-23).

For another example let us consider the offensiveness of negative gossip which, being indirectly conveyed, reaches the ears of its target, if at all, only after considerable intermediation by others. A predicament can develop only at this point, the author of which, however, will very likely remain unknown. In the course of it all the mesostructure may be modified:

> Vengeful gossip, when directed at an in-group member, can be quite disruptive of group harmony, and in many preliterate societies there are formalized and supernatural sanctions for controlling it. . . . Among the West African Ashanti, tale-bearing is considered a serious breach of etiquette that must be publicly punished. If the target is someone of high status within the tribe, the perpetrator either has his lips cut off or is executed (Rosnow and Fine, 1976: 91-92).

Conclusions

It was stated at the end of chapter 1 that predicaments, although they invariably end, can nevertheless have consequences stretching well beyond their boundaries. These consequences take three forms: revenge, avoidance, and entrapment. Still, our discussion of the nature and composition of the mesostructure indicates that the scope of a given predicament is still broader than these consequences, for adjustments of various kinds can also take place in the related mesostructure surrounding it. Moreover, these adjustments may influence subsequent behavior. In the wake of a predicament, at least five possible adjustments can be identified for the mesostructure within which it has unfolded.

One, people may become partisan, claiming on the one side that the author did nothing wrong or meant no harm, or claiming on the other side that the offended individuals were immorally treated. Two, those who are offended may refuse from thereon to work or cooperate with the author or, if they stop short of this measure and continue in the relationship, they may discover they can only function there with reduced effectiveness. Three, stories about the social undesirability of the author may spread through the larger social network or social world portraying him or her as someone who is, for instance, insulting, paranoid, unctuous, secretive, or deceitful. Four, to the extent they are viewed as being touchy, prudish, insecure, and the like, certain people may acquire a reputation for being too easily offended. Five, where authors are perceived in local circles as seriously "immoral," as people who all too frequently violate the moral precepts of etiquette, however intentional or unintentional their actions, other people who are thrown into contact with them may try to change these troublesome individuals.

For all five adjustments the long-term result is a set of new relationships or new identities or both, changes that take their place as new rules or new categories in the frames guiding behavior in the corresponding areas of social life. This reflexive circle calls attention to the broader significance of the predicament as an occurrence with far greater import in everyday life than a fleeting peeve or even a substantial irritant. Because those who are offended are now motivated to avoid further unpleasantness of this kind, predicaments can be a source of significant social change at the mesostructural level. The next seven chapters provide the empirical detail needed to illustrate this proposition as well as the others we have discussed with reference to the theoretical perspective of everyday life sociology.

References

Adler, Patricia A., Peter Adler, and Andrea Fontana. 1987. Everyday life sociology. In *Annual review of sociology*, vol. 13, edited by W. Richard Scott and James F. Short, Jr., 217-35. Palo Alto, Calif.: Annual Reviews Inc.

Ball, Donald W. 1965. Sarcasm as sociation: The rhetoric of interaction. *Canadian Review of Sociology and Anthropology* 2: 190-98.

Brissett, Dennis, and Charles Edgley (eds.). 1990. *Life as theater*, 2nd ed. New York: Aldine de Gruyter.

Cooley, Charles H. 1902. *Human nature and the social order*. New York: Schribner's.

Denzin, Norman K. 1984. *On misunderstanding emotion*. San Francisco, Calif.: Jossey-Bass.

Felson, Richard B. 1992. Self-concept. In *Encyclopedia of sociology*, vol. 4, edited by Edgar F. Borgatta and Marie L. Borgatta, 1743-49. New York: Macmillan.

Fine, Gary Alan, and Sherryl Kleinman. 1983. New work and meaning: An interactionist approach to structure. *Symbolic Interaction* 6:97-110.

Flynn, Charles P. 1977. *Insult and society*. Port Washington. N.Y.: Kennikat Press.

Franks, David. 1985. Introduction to the special issue on the sociology of emotions. *Symbolic Interaction* 8: 161-70.

Freilich, Morris. 1991. Smart rules and proper rules: A journey through deviance. In *Deviance: Anthropological perspectives*, edited by Morris Freilich, Douglas Raybeck, and Joel Savishinsky, 27-50. New York: Bergen & Garvey.

Goffman, Erving. 1967. *Interaction ritual*. Chicago: Aldine.

Goffman, Erving. 1974. *Frame analysis*. New York: Harper & Row.

Gonos, George. 1977. Situation versus frame: The interactionist and the structualist analyses of everyday life. *American Sociological Review* 42: 854-67.

Hall, Peter M. 1987. Interactionism and the study of social organization. *The Sociological Quarterly* 28: 1-22.

Harré, Rom. 1977. The ethogenic approach: Theory and practice. In *Advances in experimental social psychology*, vol. 10, edited by Leonard Berkowitz, 284-314. New York: Academic Press.

Harrington, C. Lee. 1992. Talk about embarrassment: Exploring the taboo-repression-denial hypothesis. *Symbolic Interaction* 15: 203-26.

Hochschild, Arlie R. 1983. *The managed heart.* Berkeley, Calif.: University of California Press.

Jones, Edward E. 1964. *Ingratiation.* New York: Appleton-Century-Crofts.

Lemert, Edwin M. 1972. *Human deviance, social problems, and social control*, 2nd ed. Englewood Cliffs, N.J.: Prentice-Hall.

Lindesmith, Alfred R., Anselm L. Strauss, and Norman K. Denzin. 1991. *Social psychology*, 7th ed. Englewood Cliffs, N.J.: Prentice-Hall.

Maffesoli, Michel. 1989. Editorial preface. *Current Sociology* 37 (Spring): v-vi.

Maines, David R. 1982. In search of mesostructure. *Urban Life* 11: 267-79.

Mazur, Allan. 1985. A biosocial model of status in face-to-face primate groups. *Social Forces* 64: 377-402.

McCall, George J, and J.L. Simmons. 1978. *Identities and interactions*, rev. ed. New York: Free Press.

Mead, Margaret. 1977. Jealousy: Primitive and civilized. In *Jealousy*, edited by Gordon Clanton and Lynn G. Smith, 115-28. Englewood Cliffs, N.J.: Prentice-Hall.

Rosnow, Ralph L., and Gary Alan Fine. 1976. *Rumor and gossip: The social psychology of hearsay.* New York: Elsevier.

Rossi, Alice. 1984. Gender and parenthood. *American Sociological Review* 49: 1-18.

Schneider, David J. 1981. Tactical self-presentations: Toward a broader conception. In *Impression management theory and social psychological research*, edited by James T. Tedeschi, 23-40. New York: Academic Press.

Stebbins, Robert A. 1976. *Commitment to deviance: The nonprofessional criminal in the community.* Westport, Conn.: Greenwood.

Stebbins, Robert A. 1986. The definition of the situation: A review. In *Social behavior in context*, edited by Adrian Furnham, 34-54. Boston: Allyn & Bacon.

Strauss, Anselm L. 1978. *Negotiations.* San Francisco, Calif.: Jossey-Bass.

Stryker, Sheldon. 1990. Symbolic interactionism: Themes and variations. In *Social psychology: Sociological perspectives*, edited by Morris Rosenberg and Ralph H. Turner, 3-29. New Brunswick, N.J.: Transaction.

Sugrue, Noreen M. 1982. Emotions as property and context for negotiation. *Urban Life* 11: 280-92.

Thoits, Peggy A. 1989. The sociology of emotions. In *Annual review of sociology*, vol. 15, edited by W. Richard Scott and Judith Blake, 317-42. Palo Alto, Calif.: Annual Reviews Inc.

Unruh, David. 1979. Characteristics and types of participation in social worlds. *Symbolic Interaction* 2: 115-30.

Yount, Kristen R. 1991. Ladies. flirts, and tomboys: Strategies for managing sexual harrassment in an underground coal mine. *Journal of Contemporary Ethnography* 19: 396-422.

Weigert, Andrew J. 1983. *Social psychology.* Notre Dame, Ind.: Notre Dame University Press.

Wolff, Michael. 1973. Notes on the behavior of pedestrians. In *People in places: The sociology of the familiar*, edited by Arnold Birenbaum and Edward Sagarin, 35-48. New York: Praeger.

Chapter 3

THE PUT-ON

> Excited scientists announced Wednesday they had filmed the formation of mysterious circles of flattened wheat that have appeared in England for centuries. . . .
>
> A team keeping a night vigil in a field in Wiltshire recorded flashing lights and at dawn discovered more of the circles, variously claimed to be the work of visitors from outer space, the Devil, or whirlwinds.
>
> The experts taking part in Operation Blackbird proudly announced their find to reporters as a major scientific event.
>
> Then the scientists from Britain, Japan, West Germany, and the United States, who are equipped with sophisticated monitoring equipment and helicopters, took a closer look.
>
> Inside the flattened circles they found ouija boards - commonly used in occult rituals - and crosses, apparently left behind not by little green men but very human hoaxers.
>
> A few hours after their first announcement, the crestfallen scientists appeared on BBC television, which coordinated the research project, to admit the down-to-earth truth and denonce the anonymous pranksters *Calgary Herald*, Thursday, 26 July 1990, p. A2).

Deception, as a human social activity, is neither new nor necessarily dishonored. Machiavelli, for example, once noted that "the more easily and securely the deception succeeds, the more glory and honor it gains. Hence pernicious men are praised for their ingenuity, and good men blamed as foolish." Deception has been a solid member of the repertoire of playwrights and novelists, as seen in the works of William Shakespeare and Mark Twain among many others. Even scientists must occasionally deal with a deliberately faked world as seen in the notorious Piltdown Man hoax in the first decade of this century. Early in 1974 it was hinted that the Vinland map is really a skilled forgery, while later that year falsified data were discovered in medical and parapsychological research (*Time*, 1974). David Goodrich (1973) has provided us with an often humorous but authoritative account of art fakes in America from the time of Paul Revere to the present. From literature, Farrer (1907) has assembled and annotated an impressive variety of forgeries, which have been carried out since the advent of writing. And, we marvel at the deceptive genius of spies, especially when they work for our cause.

While the practice of deception is old, the nomenclature "putting someone on" and "put-on" are new. Evidently, they emerged in the underside of American life around 1964, particularly in collegiate circles (*Harpers Bazaar*, 1965:173; *New York Times*, 1965:20). Since that time these notions have moved into the mainstream of polite conversation to a degree sufficient to earn an entry in *Webster's New Collegiate Dictionary*. One effect of this linguistic addition is that such common forms of deception as being sent on a snipe hunt, or to fetch a fallopian tube, left-handed monkey wrench, or sky hook, which appear to be somewhat older, have been relabeled as put-ons.

But, putting people on is more than the old styles of deception dressed up in new clothes. It is, as Jacob Brackman (1971:17-18) points out, a new mode of communication in American society; it is deceptive behavior that goes beyond the traditional practices of "funning," kidding, or teashing. It is more subtle, as I intend to show, and much more pervasive culturally (e.g., now in politics and science) than these older practices.

The put-on and the process of putting someone on are, then, new colloquialisms referring to intentionally and successfully misleading acts (or products) directed by one or more persons at one or more others. Examination of the definitions of these terms offered in *Webster's Diction-aries* (Unabridged and New Collegiate editions), in the *Oxford English Dictionary*, in two thesauruses of slang (Wentworth and Flexner, 1967:414, 700; Berry and Van Den Bark, 1953:301, 359), and in descriptions from a group of university students of put-ons they had either witnessed or been directly involved in, suggests three motives for engaging in such behavior.[1]

One motive is the put-on perpetrated by the *deceiver* on the *mark* - the object of the put-on - for fun or sport. Putting someone on can be a form of amusement or diversion. Another motive for putting people on is either to test their ability to discriminate sincere acts or products of a given type from insincere acts or products or to demonstrate their inability. The third motive for putting others on is to achieve some sort of profit or gain, which may be monetary or nonmonetary, such as a gain in self-regard, self-protection, competitive advantage, privilege, compliance by others, or some other personal end. As pure types, the last two motives betray a seriousness on the part of the deceiver, largely absent in the first.

The remainder of this paper deals with the general nature of put-ons and the social psychology of putting on our fellowman. The principal source of data for observations made in these sections is a set of 101 put-ons collected from 77 university students. They were asked to record on paper, in as much detail as they could remember, occasions in which they have been put-on, perpetrated a put-on, or observed one. The author's experiences with put-ons in art, science, literature, and everyday life have been used to extend further this empirical base. No attempt is made here to examine in detail the many specific forms of put-ons, on some of which there has already been a great deal written under other names. Rather my interest is in the behavioral manifestations of this idea and their broader social correlates.

The Nature of Put-ons

One of the first discoveries in conducting the library research portion of this paper was that American English is rich in words denoting forms and near forms of deception. Portraying the nature of put-ons can be effectively carried out by relating them to these kindred terms. Three types of put-ons based on the three motives offer a convenient framework for this task.

The *sporting* put-on is possibly the most frequent of the three types. At least my sample listed over twice as many of them as they did *profitable* put-ons, the second most numerous type. There are times when the sporting put-on is also a practical joke, a joke whose humor stems from the tricking or abuse of an individual placed somehow at a disadvantage. The following incident reported by one of the respondents illustrates the combination of practical joking and putting someone one for fun:

> One Friday afternoon about four o'clock I decided I would go to my room to rest for a few minutes before taking a shower and going out for the usual Friday night activities. I soon fell asleep, only to be awakened by my two roommates who were urging me to hurry up, shower, and get dressed so that we could go out for the evening. So, as fast as I could, I took the shower, dressed, went downstairs for a quick beer, and announced I was ready to go. The three of us went outside to the car where I noticed that there was an unusually small amount of activity for what must have been nine o'clock on a Friday night. When I mentioned this my friends could hold back no longer; I had made a great effort to go out for the evening at three o'clock in the morning.

Other practical jokes fail to qualify as put-ons because they involve no deception. The tack on the chair, the hot foot, the short-sheeted bed, and similar antics are examples. The sporting put-on is equivalent to kidding someone, when kidding does not refer to ribbing or teasing. Though, in kidding, we are likely to let the mark in on his deception, whereas there is a tendency to avoid this when putting him on (Brackman, 1971:18).

The least frequent of the three types was the *discriminative* put on. It is often emanated from the desire to have fun as well as the desire to test another person's judgmental ability. Familiar examples were mentioned by the respondents, such as seasoned enlisted men testing the expertise of a freshly minted second lieutnant or late adolescent boys in a psychiatric hospital feigning the stereotyped symptoms of mental illness before a student nurse in order to assess the sophistication of her training. A handful of the discriminative put-ons reported were, however, deadly serious.

Sociologists have recently been made aware of a couple of purely discriminative put-ons. A plagiarized article printed some twenty years ago was submitted to five leading journals to ascertain whether the editors and reviewers would spot its true nature (Snell, 1973). A similar test is reported in the *Subterranean Sociological Newsletter* (1970:3) concerning an earlier article printed in an American sociological periodical. Discriminative put-ons are also found in music where, on occasion, symphony orchestra musicians deliberately feign incompetence (e.g., playing out of tune, out of rhythm, in the wrong place) to see if a new or guest conductor is alert and skillful enough to notice it (Robert R. Faulkner, personal communication).

The *profitable* put-on covers a range of ideas in American English denoting or connoting deception for some sort of personal gain. They include the following, some of which are ciminal: the tall tale, comeon, setup, hoax, hypocrisy, hustle (or swindle in, for example, pool or prison), imposture (pretense, cheat, fraud, fake, quack), forgery, and ingratiation (c.f., Jones, 1964). The come-on is possibly the only relatively unfamiliar form in this list. The following incident, reported by one respondent, illustrates the come-on, or how one person can induce another, through deception, to behave in a way that the other would ordinarily resist and that is profitable to the deceiver:

> A put-on I often use when dating a new girl is to tell her I've had an illegitimate son. I act very embarrassed and hurt, with the result that the girl thinks she knows a deep secret of my life. She then opens up to me about herself.

Like the discriminative put-on, the profitable form sometimes springs from the sporting motive as well. This appears especially likely in the perpetration of some tall tales, come-ons, impostures, and forgeries.

The Social Psychology of Putting People On

Outside Erving Goffman's work, sociologists and social psychologists have paid scant attention to the place of deception in everyday life. Psychologists have focused primarily on deception in experiments, as cheating a college and secondary school classrooms, and to a lesser degree, as manifested in lying. Sociologists, when they have shown any interest, have been as concerned with the unwitting and often unavoidable deception of social interaction as with the intentional variety - the focus of this paper. Nevertheless, my observations, reports from the sample, and discussions with colleagues and friends, indicate that the process of putting others on offers a rich source of social psychological data.

Putting people on is examined from three angles in this section: social interaction, social identity, and social situation.

Social Interaction

Our definition of the process of putting people on is, in a way, an objective one: the deceiver intentionally and *successfully* misleads the mark, whatever either party thinks the outcome is. The objective aspect calls attention to the fact that some proportion of acts or products intended to deceive someone else fail; they are *attempted* put-ons. The well-known phrase, "putting on airs," seems to refer to attempted put-ons by those who are identified as acting affectedly or ostentatiously. Their effort at imposturing as sophisticated has been unsuccessful, and they are seen by others present as putting on airs.

There is also some benefit to be gained from viewing a put-on subjectively or from the standpoint of those concerned. Discussion here is fruitfully organized in terms of Glaser and Strauss' (1964) four awareness contests, developed originlly from their observations on awareness of dying.

Put-ons that are never discovered by the mark or discovered only after they are completed occur in a "closed awareness" context: the mark fails to realize he is being put on. He has been successfully mislead.

In the "suspected awareness" context, the mark does not know for sure, but suspects he is being put on. One reaction that may discourage completing a deception as it is unfolding (unless it is a phony physical product the manufacture of which is hidden from the mark) is to question the deceiver directly with some such remark as: Are you putting me on?" If this fails to stop him, he is faced with the task of attempting to complete the put-on directed at a mark who is exceptioinally alert to signs of insincerity. For various reasons, the mark may decide to go along with the deceiver's sham, in which case a "mutual pretense" context may develop; both mark and deceiver know the latter is putting the former on, but pretend otherwise.

It is in the suspected awareness context that connoisseurs of culture (art, music, film, fashion, etc.) have, in recent years, developed an interesting protective strategy. Fearful of the possibility that avantgarde products in these spheres may be put-ons, they adopt a superficially sophisticated tolerance toward them (Brackman, 1971:31-33). They are saying, in effect, "I don't especially like this stuff, but I will forbear having it around since there is the chance it is genuine art." This is a safe noncommittal stance characteristic of all tolerance; the viewer or listener neither embraces nor scorns the work - he is neither put on nor insulting to the creator (c.f., Stebbins, 1971). Or, as Burton Hillis puts it: "I have finally learned what to say at an avant-garde art show. If I don't like a painting, it's interesting; if I really hate it, it's provocative."

Attempted put-ons, though they may start in a closed awareness context, fizzle because the mark catches on. He converts the situation to an "open awareness" contest where both he and the deceiver know he is being put on.

The suspected awareness context can lead, on occasion, to what may be called the *false* put-on: one believes another is intentionally deceiving him, when, in fact, he is not. False put-ons issue from, among others, misunderstandings of human signs and symbols and from mistaken identities. The following incident, reported by one of our respondents, illustrates how a mistaken identity can generate a false put-on:

> Recently, my roommate who is from India and myself stopped at a gas station in Dallas. It was run by two Mexicans; one could speak English, the other only a few words. As we came to a stop, the former, though he knows English, began to speak to us in Spanish. He had seen my roommate and assumed he was Mexican. I answered in Spanish telling him *we* do not understand that language and can speak only a few sentences. He started to laugh and called his partner over. They were convinced this was a put-on; my roommate was really Mexican. Throughout the subsequent conversation they kept reverting to Spanish in order to trick him into answering in his presumed native language and thus reveal his true identity. My roommate, who is very shy just sat there dazed by it all.

In the bulk of those put-ons that root, in whole or in part, in the sporting motive, the deceiver is performing his deception before an *audience*: those present in the situation whose opinions of his behavior there he values.[2] It is the deceiver's hope that, for succeeding in putting someone on, he will be viewed by the audience as a wit, life of the party, good-time Charley, or some such gratifying imputation. For this to occur the audience must somehow be in the know, which means that the mark can only be in the audience or comprise the audience when he is let in on the deception following its completion. The audience, of course, need not be physically present. They may be told of the put-on at some later occasion from which the mark is absent. However and whenever the audience gains knowledge of it, the put-on is a form of private joke consumed among a group of insiders or sophisticates and perpetrated by one of their number.[3]

Whether the deceiver actually receives the approbation of the audience, depends upon the appropriateness of his deception and its target. Some matters are too serious to be treated with levity. Some people are too important or too sensitive to be selected as marks.

The question of the appropriateness of a put-on suggests that it is rarely a happy event for everyone. This is obvious for most, if not all, discriminative and profitable put-ons, but it is also true of the sporting variety. In other words, in every put-on the deceiver is benefiting in some way at the expense of the mark. Even if the mark never learns of the deception, the deceiver and audience know. With them, he has lost something, usually a degree of respect, for having been gullible, unsophisticated, or undiscriminating enough to be misled. However slightly, the mark's relations with some members of his social world have changed - usually for the worse.

If and when the mark learns he has been put on, whether he learns immediately after completion of the sham or later, embarrassment appears to be the nearly universal reaction. Embarrassment, Goffman (1956:265) observes, "has to do with the figure the individual cuts before others felt to be there at the time. The crucial concern is the impression one makes on others in the present." As the target of a put-on, the mark is embarrassed because his public image as reasonably perceptive and worldly-wise has been tarnished in some degree. He has been taken or played for a sucker; he thus loses poise in the situation in that he no longer has the same degree of control over his presentation of self he did earlier (c.f., Gross and Stone, 1964).

There are, of course, certain situations in which the mark actually suffers little or no embarrassment. Little embarrassment should result from being deceived about highly technical matters that the mark has no chance of being conversant with. And, in some circles one or two pathetic individuals can only gain entrance to them if they accept the role of laughing stock. To the extent that they identify with his status, they should experience no embarrassment from being made a mark. Finally, there are situations, normally collective, where we expect to be put-on and thus entertained. The comedy show, circus, and magician's performance are examples. This suggests, that, in general, embarrassment is probably reduced considerably when many people in the situation are made marks.

Sometimes embarrassment is the less poignant of two emotional reactions to being put on, the other reaction being relief. One gullible freshman in the Reserve Officers Training Corps was even more relieved than embarrassed when told he no longer had to learn how to conduct the flag raising ceremonies by early the next morning. His associates took pity on him and divulged that they were putting him on about his role in this detail. A few respondents also mentioned that they became angry with the deceiver for putting them on.

But, embarrassment is the most frequent emotional concomitant of putting someone on. The deceiver, when discovered, is felt by the mark to be treacherous. He has betrayed the trust the mark had originally put in him to work, as others are expected to do, to prevent embarrassment from overtaking anyone in the situation. Now the deceiver has deliberately worked the mark into a psychologically uncomfortable position in order to achieve some form of personal benefit.[4]

Indeed, the potential for embarrassment that any put-on holds is one criterion the audience may use in judging the appropriateness of such an act. The risk a would-be deceiver faces who finds himself in a suspected awreness context with a potential mark is that *he* (the deceiver) may be embarrassed because he is unable to pull off the deception. He will be embarrassed because he is unable to deceive the mark successfully and because he has been discovered engaging in treacherous interpersonal behavior. Once put on, a mark is likely to be more cautious about what he accepts as sincere from the deceiver. So, like the shepherd boy who cried wolf too often, the deceiver may find it more difficult either to deceive the mark again or to convince him of actual fact (false put-ons). Furthermore, he must now be prepared for a counter-put-on from the mark who may be eager to retaliate. The possibility of mutual, enduring disbelief appears in such a situation, as two would-be deceivers try to make marks of each other while avoiding the same fate themselves. In fact, past transactions in the present situation and in earlier ones may now be retrospectively reinter-preted as possible put-ons. A specimen from one respondent demonstates well the roles of embarrassment, counter-put-on, and mutual disbelief in the social psychology of deception:

One weekend I went to my boyfriend's parents' house to spend a few days with them. We were supposed to have gotten back early Sunday afternoon, but failed to for various reasons. A friend of mine called my house several times throughout the day in an effort to reach me. Knowing she would be curious about this weekend visit, I decided to call her and pretend that we had gotten married. I carried the story out for nearly thirty minutes. At that point I told her the truth because she tends to gossip a lot. She was embarrassed for having believed my story.

A few days later she told me about how this guy she was dating got mad at her and made her get out of his car and walk home. She explained how she called her relatives in Dallas and had them come to a telephone booth to pick her up. At first, I thought this was unbelievable, but eventually I accepted the story as true. As the day went on she continued to talk about the incident, and it gradually dawned on me that she was putting me on probably to get even with me for putting her on earlier.

Social Identities and Social Situations

Among the many social identities people hold, some have also gained a reputation as *inveterate* deceivers who routinely engage in one or more of the three types of put-ons. There is evidence from our sample that inveterate deceivers, whatever their motives, take a noticeable amount of pride in their skills of deceit. Skills notwithstanding, their endeavors are aided by having individual around who are known for their gullibility. While the inveterate deceiver undoubtedly finds that his reputation serves to restrain the practice of his art, there are circumstances that prevent it from completely obstructing his schemes.[5]

One of these is that people are perhaps most easily put on in connection with strongly held values, beliefs, goals, and desires. There are many events they would like to see take place, which, when told that one of these has, in fact, happened, they are inclined to accept the account with only cursory examination. The attractiveness to some of objectively phony ingratiation and role supportive put-ons is obvious here. Attempted put-ons that run counter to our cherished aims and views, it may be hypothesized, are more critically scrutinized, with the result that, for the deception to succeed, the deceiver must call up considerable ingenuity.

Another circumstance that aids the deceiver in putting others on is the technical richness of so many areas of modern life. Any expert is in a position to put on these unacquainted with his field.

Concerning sporting put-ons among adults, the data suggest that such deceivers are more often male than female. Further, males seem to select females as marks as often as other males; while females, when they act as deceivers, are more likely to select another female instead of a male. Males were commonly the ones identified as inveterate deceivers, rarely females. An interesting question for further research, on which I have no data, is whether those gullible persons who are frequent marks engage in much putting on of their own. Their own empathy for other marks might preclude such deception.

Turning to the situational aspects of putting people on, it may be noted that deceptions of this sort are easiest to perpetrate and hence most likely to occur in secondary relations. Sociologists from Simmel onward have recognized that interpersonal relationships are built on, among other things, a tendency to gain total knowledge about the other person. This sort of information about a would-be deceiver makes it difficult for him to put on such an individual. That put-ons do occur among husbands and wives and among friends, whatever the sex, does not necessarily invalidate this observation. Such behavior does suggest that the relationships are not as developed as they could be, not only because there is considerably less than total knowledge of the partner, but also beause one partner, at least, does not empathize enough with the other to care whether he embarrasses him should he learn of the deception.

If putting on others thrives in secondary settings, then cities should spawn more of such behavior than the countryside. Still, ruralists and villagers are not above putting on city folks about, for example, how rustic they are or how rough their daily existence is. These practices, however, take place in secondary relations.

CONCLUSIONS

We have been concerned here with the who, what, when, where, and why of putting people on. How it is done has received no systematic treatment here, for it is a subject complicated enough to occupy at least one separate paper (for a start, see Brackman, 1971).

What is the place of the put-on in everyday life and in society? I have spoken of the pernicious effects of willful deception upon the hapless mark who, if he becomes aware of it, suffers embarrassment, but at times, there are even worse alternatives than deception. Social scientists, such as Simmel (1950), Goffman (1959), and McCall and Simmons (1966), have long recognized the occasional necessity of secrecy and deception in the presentation of an acceptable self. So important it is that certain aspects of our lives remain hidden from view, that people in social encounters join with each other in avoiding situations wherein someone will be forced to reveal these dark secrets. Deliberate impostures and even some ingratiations, as profitable put-ons, make life more tolerable for certain individuals, while harming little those who are taken in by them.

Children in American society are taught about the virtures of honesty and straightforwardness and the sins of deception and lying. Only later, as young adults, do they come to make finer judgments about the appropriateness of these practices in the maze of everyday affairs. No one teaches us how to make these judgments. Rather, we are left with the general principles of good honesty and bad deception to figure out how they really articulate with one another in our lives and those of our associates. So intricate is this articulation that it is doubtful it could be effectively communicated in any other way than through the slow process of experience.

Yet, even experience as teacher leaves something to be desired here. Experience seems not have taught some of us that enacting put-ons, especially the sporting variety, chills social relations. Those who put others on with any regularity give evidence that they are not *warm* persons. Warm persons, according to Lofland (1969:273-274), appear to care about others as full persons or whole beings. They appear to project themselves as genuine and sincere. Warm persons avoid toying with the self-conceptions of their fellows. People who put others on for fun give the impression of being happy souls without a care in the world. This may be true. And they may, in other ways, be warm persons, in that they are unreseved and understanding. Putting people on, particularly for kicks, is inconsistent with this sort of orientation toward mankind.

Men who need to present false fronts and preserve dark secrets about themselves need also to maintain distance between themselves and others (see Simmel, 1950: 315-316). Put-ons of all types can aid them in this effort. Men who have relatively few such needs would do well by themselves to avoid putting on their fellowman. Though they may not know it, such behavior is out of character for them, since they generally ten to avoid the use of deception.

Endnotes

1. The older and foreign sources are useful in helping distinguish the most recent, hip, use of these phrases from their more established relatives.

2. The definition of audience is identical to that presented by Goffman 1961:85- 152) in his essay on role distance. Taking role distance, by the way, should not be confused with putting someone on. Role distance behavior is an attempt to preserve one's self-esteem by psychologically

removing oneself from certain distasteful role requirements. There is nothing deceiving about such behavior; at least the actor intends no deception. It is an ingroup form of communication he uses to inform those reference others who are present (the audience) of his dislike for the requirments, a dislike they expect him to harbor. Those outside these esoteric circles are not being deceived, only excluded from a private message.

3. It is possible that, in some circumstances, such as when men put on their wives or girlfriends, the deceiver is his own audience or the audience is imaginary.

4. Embarrassment mixed with the intent to socialize or control someone (Gross and Stone, 1964) is often part of the overall aim of the deceiver enacting a discriminative put-on.

5. He can always adopt the strategy of one inveterate deceiver in the sample. He reports the truth in such a way as to lead others to believe they are about to become marks. He interlards his genuine put-ons with false ones.

References

Berry, Lester V. and Melvin Van Den Bark
   1953   The American Thesaurus of Slang, 2nd ed. New York: Crowell.

Brackman, Jacob
   1971   The Put-On. Chicago: Henry Regnery.

Farrer, J.A.
   1907   Literary Forgeries. New York: Longmans Green.

Glaser, Barney G. and Anselm L. Strauss
   1964   Awareness of Dying. Chicago: Aldine.

Goffman, Erving
   1956   "Embarrassment and social organization." American Journal
          of Sociology 62. (November): 264-274
   1959   The Presentation of Self in Everyday Life. Garden City, New
          York: Doubleday.
   1961   Encounters, Indianapolis: Bobbs-Merrill.

Goodrich, David L.
1973   Art Fakes in America. New York: Viking

Gross, Edward and Gregory P. Stone
1964   "Embarrassment and the analysis of role requirements." American Journal of Sociology 70 (July): 1-15.

Harpers Bazaar
1965   (April)

Jones, Edward E.
1964   Ingratiation. New York: Appleton-Century-Crofts.

Lofland, John
1969   Deviance and Identity. Englewood Cliffs, N.J.: Prentice Hall.

McCall, George J. and J. L. Simmons
1966   Identities and Interactions. New York: Free Press.

New York Times
1965   December 27.

Simmel, Georg
1950   The Sociology of Georg Simmel. Trans. By Kurt Wolff. New York: Free Press.

Snell, Joel C.
1973   "Editorial standards and authenticity of manuscripts." American Sociologist 8 (May): 90-91.

Stebbins, Robert A.
1974   "The nature and development of tolerance." Behavioral Sciences Tape Library (3-hour casette) (Fort Lee, N.J.: Sigma Information).

Subterranean Sociological Newsletter
1970   4(May): 3.

Time
1974   103(February 4): 12; (April 29): 67; (August 26): 74-75.

Wentworth, Harold and Stuart B. Flexner, eds.
1967   Dictionary of American Slang. New York: Crowell.

Chapter 4

SELFISHNESS

This is the true joy in life, the being used for a purpose recognized by yourself as a mighty one; the being thoroughly worn out before you are thrown on the scrap heap; the being a force of nature instead of a feverish selfish little clod of ailments and grievances complaining that the world will not devote itself to making you happy (George Bernard Shaw, *Man and Superman* [epistle dedicatory]).

Selfishness is viewed here as a fact of everyday life and a disagreeable one at that. In terms of common sense the moral standing of selfishness is clear: 'It is one of the most generally agreed judgements of ordinary morality that unselfishness is to be commended and selfishness condemned' (Downie and Telfer, 1969:39). Broadly put, 'selfish' is an imputation most commonly hurled at perceived self-seekers by their victims, where the self-seekers are seen to demonstrate a concern for their own welfare or advantage at the expense of or in disregard for those victims. The present study suggests we tend to use the term to describe someone else's actions and only rarely to describe our own, owing perhaps to the ethical implications involved.

The central thread of selfishness is its exploitative unfairness - a kind of personal favoritism that infects our daily affairs. Yet, selfishness fails to qualify as 'deviance' as sociologists routinely use this term. As an act, selfishness is located on a different moral plane from, say, homocide, compulsive gambling, or even nudism or marijuana smoking. It is a transgression of the folkways or, more to the point, of certain rules of etiquette and courtesy (cf., Cooley, 1922:216).

*This paper was presented as part of the Maurice Manel Lectureship, Atkinson College, York University, 23 February 1978. I wish to thank Arthur W. Frank, III, for his support and scholarly advice throughout the project.

Professor Hockart (1931:615) defines etiquette as the body of norms of conventional decorum or manners into which one's behavior is cast. The reasons for studying these seemingly minor ceremonial rules of daily life are set out by Goffman (1963:5-10; 1967:53-6) and need not be reviewed here.[1] Other common breaches of etiquette have already attracted the attention of social psychologists, among them: embarrassment, deference, and demeanour (e.g., Goffman, 1967); modesty, pride, and conceit (Stebbins, 1972;1976); jealousy (Clanton and Smith, 1977); privacy (e.g., Schwartz, 1968; Lofland, 1973); and situational ignorance (e.g., Stebbins, 1975a).[2]

Whatever the reason, selfishness has been all but ignored by social scientists. The aim of the present paper is to correct this deficiency, first by examining the nature of adult selfishness and then by exploring its manifestations in routine social interaction. The role of power in selfishness is also discussed as is the possibility that excessive selfishness is a personality blemish for some people. The empirical background for these ideas comes from eighty-eight cases of selfishness reported by sixty-seven student respondents in an upper-division sociology course.[3]

The Nature of Selfishness

We may start by elaborating on the definition of selfishness just presented. At the risk of stressing the obvious, it should be noted that a selfish act is necessarily a goal-directed one. Self-seekers have certain ends in mind, the pursuit of which results in what others define as unfair exploitation. Nevertheless, we shall see that they may be surprised, even chagrined, to learn that their purposive behaviour has been defined by its victim as self-centered.

The earlier definition, in its one-sentence simplicity, suggests that the victim loses something in this unhappy exchange with the self-seeker. More precisely, victims impute selfishness where they fail to benefit as expected. A refusal to share some valued item is often at issue:

> My sister got a book for Christmas that I wanted to read. She said I could do this after she had finished. Well, she finished reading it two days before I had to return it to the university. I asked if I could take it back with me. My other sister would be coming to visit me the following week so that she could return it when she left. But my first sister was selfish; she wouldn't let me borrow the book for, at most, three weeks, even after she had already read it. When I asked why, she replied 'because.' That's selfish. Because of her selfish act. . . I will have to wait until next summer [to read the book.]

The antithesis of selfishness, which is self-sacrifice, gives us further insight into its nature. In self-sacrifice one's person or interest is surrendered for others or for some cause or ideal. It contains 'breadth and magnanimity,' as Cooley (1922:220) put it, in contrast to the 'narrowness' of the self-seeker's orientation.

This leads to a consideration of certain beavioural neighbours, or what selfishness is not. Nathaniel Branden's (1961:57) belief that altruism is the logical opposite of selfishness (or egoism as he prefers it) is inaccurate. It overlooks the fact that we can be altruistic without engaging in self-sacrifice. Altruism is the uncalculated consideration of, regard for, or devotion to others' interests. One could act altruistically by urging the government to tax the rich to give to the poor. If that individual were in the middle class, he or she would have surrendered nothing in making this altruistic appeal.

Branden collaborated with Ayn Rand in *The Virtue of Selfishness* to develop an ethical view of this attitude that diverges sharply from conventional usage, on which the present paper concentrates. Their work is mentioned here simply to identify one analytic route we shall avoid. Rand (1961:X) defines selfishness as 'concern with one's own interest,' which is virtuous because it is a 'rational self-interest' not one that is whimisical, emotional, or expressed at the expense, disregard, or disadvantage of others. Her 'Objectivist ethics' holds that actors must always be the beneficiary of their own actions. Exploiting others to reach this end is shortsighted; it fails to achieve happiness or achieve the actor's own values. It makes the person a parasite. But the commonsensical usage of 'selfishness' fails to recognize such philosophic distinctions. And it is commonsensical usage that intrigues the social psychologist, for that is what he encounters in everyday social relations.

Our conception of selfishness also differs from the rational pursuit of self-interest, which is occasionally cited as an important motive in economic activities (e.g., Parsons, 1940). In economic self-interest the concern is with one's own material well-being and whatever advantage is required to accomplish this. Obviously, some self-interest is also selfish since it unfairly exploits others in some way. Under these conditions selfishness is but part of a broader, more complex transaction.

Finally, it should be understood that, in everyday usage, 'selfishness' seems to refer only to breaches of etiquette, even though our definition could be applied to the behavior of a rapist or thief. We seldom describe rape or theft as selfish. Rather, stronger adjectives are chosen to express our moral outrage, such as 'sick,' 'depraved,' 'vicious,' or 'degenerate.'

Social Interaction

Selfishness, as previously stated, is an ethical imputation that is constructed in reaction to an executed or projected act of another person. Someone is believed to have violated, or to be contemplating a violation of, the rules of propriety that guide the pursuit of our personal interests *vis-à-vis* those around us. An imputation of selfishness, in the typical instance, is initially part of the victim's definition of the situation only, though under certain circumstances it may also comprise part of the self-seeker's definition.[4]

The goal-oriented act of selfishness communicates a more consequential message to the victim than the self-seeker realizes. The victim senses the strength of the self-seekers's aims and that person's desire to reach the goals even at the victim's expense. He also glimpses the self-seeker's image of him as a person who is powerless, inferior, blind to exploitation, unworthy of fair treatment or some other humiliating reflection. Given this interpretation, the victim has good reason to define the situation as selfishness:

> An old boyfriend of mine was very selfish. When he wanted to see me he would phone and ask me to take the bus to his place. We lived very far apart, and he did have a car. He used to make sure I left his apartment for home in time to catch the last bus of the evening. He said he didn't want to pick me up because he shared the car with his roommates. My feelings were that he should have arranged to get the car when he wanted to see me (as he did to go downtown and the like). In my opinion the reason he didn't want to pick me up was so he would not have to fill the car with gas or drive to my house and back. I eventually stopped seeing him.

In *naive selfishness* the self-seeker defines the situation in quite other ways, as if nothing were amiss. The act that is perceived by the victim as selfish is perceived by the self-seeker as ordinary goal-directed behaviour. At the theoretical or objective level Cooley (1922:217,221) identified the underlying problem as inaccurate or nonexistent role taking. Self-seekers fail to put themselves in the victim's place; they fail to see the victim's definition of the situation, particularly that person's conclusion that the behaviour in question is selfish. They are unaware of the victim's bitter thoughts about power differentials, their callousness toward the victim's interests; they do not realize imputations that they are unconcerned about and consider themselves superior to the victim. In short, self-seekers intend no such consequences. It is from the victim's standpoint that they are inconsiderate or thoughtless.

In *justifiable selfishness*, however, self-seekers are aware that the effects of their present or future actions may be unfavourably regarded. On the chance that they may be called to account for them, they prepare a defense that they hope will neutralize their self-interested behaviour (Lyman and Scott, 1970:113-14, 120-4). They may claim, for example, that they are really not selfish, for the victim would do the same if given the opportunity. Or the victim has previously been selfish to the self-seeker or others, either of which justifies the self-seeker's present behaviour; it is a sort of settling of scores. Self-seekers might contend that the victim is really little victimized or that their substantial gain vindicates the victim's 'slight' loss. It is here that selfishness also enters the self-seeker's definition of the situation.

Confrontation

Once the self-seeker's intentions are known to the victim, the next move lies with the latter. Having defined oneself as unfairly treated, one is now motivated to confront the self-seeker in an attempt to redress the injustice or prevent its recurrence. But confrontation can be risky as some respondents realized; it has both advantages and disadvantages. As the following case involving two male roommates suggests, one disadvantage is the potential interpersonal friction that is generated from such enounters:

> A former roommate of mine had a bad habit of monopolizing the couch in the living room. It was the only couch available and the most advantageous point from which to watch TV and stretch out, other than the floor. Although this selfish habit was somewhat trivial, I felt it a matter of courtesy at least to offer the couch to me occasionally. This never did occur, though there were times when its comfort would have been appreciated. Not wanting to create an inharmonious environment, I was inclined to brush it off. . .

Yet, in several cases, the reluctance to confront the self-seeker also ultimately threatened the stability, even the existence, of the interpersonal relationship. In preference to a direct encounter with the self-seeker, some victims indicated that they simply began to avoid that individual or the situation in which his or her self-centred behaviour occurred. Even if the relationship continued, the loss of respect for the self-seeker often seriously jeopardized its warmth and trust.[5]

By contrast, confrontation, though it sometimes ended in an acrimonious standoff lead, in other cases, to an exchange of views and a deeper understanding of the other person's aims and feelings. The relationship was saved, perhaps even strengthened, as a result of open discussion.

In the typical case the social dynamics of confrontation unfold as follows: A comment from the victim, such as 'Isn't that selfish?' challenges the self-seekers to defend their actions. If theirs is justifiable selfishness, their defense is already prepared and they present it. Naively selfish persons, in response to such an affront, build their defenses on the spot. Regardless of type of selfishness, victims and self-seekers now face a situation whose very social reality is open to negotiation.

Four conditions must be met before negotiation can take place (Martin, 1976: 10).

1) At least two people must be involved.

2) At least one of them must sense disagreement on how the situation should be defined.

3) No one in the situation should have the power to make his or her definition of it stick. In our case, self-seekers believe they have the power to enact the behaviour that the victim considers selfish, but not the power to make their definition of it stick as justifiable.

4) At least one person must hope to make his definition stick. These conditions pertain in the typical confrontation over selfishness.

During negotiation self-seekers challenge the imputation that their behaviour is selfish, while victims try to make that imputation stick. Whether the selfishness is naive or justifiable, negotiation revolves about the acceptability of the self-seeker's defense (planned or ad hoc) *vis-à-vis* that persons's aims in the situation and the aims of the victim. To wit, the fairness of the act is disputed.

Though the written cases gave little detail of this process, its outcomes could be clearly classified as one of three kinds. Frequently, the negotiating pair arrived at a *standoff*. Victims remained convinced they were victims; self-seekers remained convinced their self-interested behaviour was justifiable (i.e., not selfish). At other times negotiation ended on the note that the self-seeker's behaviour was *just*; the victim was, in the final analysis, no victim at all. But it also hapened that some victims won their point, developing a consensus that the self-seeker's actions were *unjust* and forcing an apology from that individual and, perhaps, a promise never again to behave that way. The following cases illustrate the first and third outcomes, respectively:

> I have been accused of freeloading off my parents and of being selfish in this way. I receive free room, board, and transportation from my parents while I'm in school. I do a minimum of chores around their house and acreage. The rest of the time I study. My parents ask for repayment in the form of work, which interferes with my studying. Thus I cannot oblige them. They accuse me of selfishly enjoying the 'luxury of an education'

at their expense. They do not pay my tuition. I have tried harder to work around the house, but it is not helping much. So I ignore the charges.

One night I came home late, and upon finding myself ravenously hungry, I searched the refrigerator. Over a quart of milk fell victim, leaving none for the morning breakfast. I was accused of being selfish by my family for this act. I didn't consider the need they had of milk for breakfast cereal in the morning. I apologized and said I wouldn't do this again.

Possibly as common as the post factum confrontation of selfishness that we have been considering is the antecedent confrontation. Here the projected acts of would-be self-seekers are challenged by would-be victims in an attempt to head off their own 'unfair' exploitation. The cases containing antecedent confrontations suggest that negotiation takes place here as well and proceeds along lines similar to those found in confrontations after the fact. And some planned selfish acts were cancelled (or at least postponed) as a result of this open dialogue, while others were carried off as the self-seekers 'got their way.'

Mutual selfishness, where both persons view themselves as victims and the other as self-seeker, always involves an antecedent confrontation. The outcome is either a standoff or a compromise, as the pair decide how to allocate a scarce value in which they both have an interest. In the first outcome, of course, the value remains unallocated for the time being:

Recently my husband and I had to make a decision which I feel involved his being selfish and also myself. The situation was one in which we had allotted a certain sum of money for the purchase of a car for me. We had been looking at secondhand cars for about a month when he had the opportunity to invest in some real estate. Of course, the money for the car was needed. He consulted with me, and I feel he did not have the least reluctance in sacrificing the car, which I had been eagerly waiting for. Initially, I saw him as being selfish in even considering suggesting this to me. But I was also [being seen by him as] selfish in refusing to give up something which had been agreed upon (the car) for something unexpected. The car was something real for me, whereas the real estate, though more beneficial to our economic unity, was not tangible. We resolved the situation by purchasing neither a car nor a piece of real estate.

In another case compromise came after a young man and woman who were courting charged each other with self-centred monopolization of personal free time. Each felt the other spent too little time with him (or her). In the end they agreed that 'each should give a little' on this matter.

Mutual selfishness grows more complicated when individuals get caught in a conflict of loyalties, wherein they discover that as they engage in self-sacrificing activity for one person or group they are indicted for selfishness by another. Building on the courtship of the preceding paragraph, it could happen that she must leave him for the afternoon to do volunteer work at a drop-in centre. But he defines this as a selfish use of time that is rightfully his. The strain caused by this imperfect meshing of roles is only exacerbated when the ethical issue of self-centredness is raised.[6]

Still another observation remains to be made on the interactive aspects of selfishness: occasionally there are *bystanders* who observe the selfish act and the confrontation that follows it (or precedes it, in projected selfishness). They, too, tend to pass judgment on the reasonableness of the imputation and the defense launched against it. They may be asked to support the victim's or the self-seeker's definition of the situation. In the event of a standoff they may serve as a sort of court of appeal. A mother exemplified still another bystander role when she acted as a conciliator in a selfishness confrontation between her two daughters.

Power

From one perspective an executed or projected act of selfishness can be understood as an expression of the power self-seekers have over their victims in the situation in which the act takes place. They manipulate 'scarce' values to their advantage and at the expense of each victim. This value, the cases show, is desired by both victim and self-seeker. And practically anything can be selfishly value: money, automobiles, food, clothing, space, athletic equipment, services, time and so on. When they impute selfishness victims are unable to obtain these values in the immediate present, because the more powerful self-seeker also desires them and they are effectively unavailable at the moment anywhere else.

The cases reported by the respondents centered almost entirely on selfishness in primary relationships involving friends and family. Casual observation suggests, however, that people are just as selfish, perhaps more so, in secondary relationships. Familiar examples abound: stealing the course notes of the best student in class to heighten one's chance of passing and to reduce competition from the note-taker; striding to the front of the queue at a cinema to save time and assure access to a good seat. One respondent related the following instance of employer selfishness:

> I am employed in a business to work from 8:30 to 5:00. Normally, if you work overtime in any job you would be paid extra. In a busy day the managers can make a margin of surplus profit by staying open an extra half hour. This particular instance happened three times. It was a very busy day and customers were still arriving at 5:30. We closed finally at 5:45. Come pay day, an extra half hour pay was included at *regular* rates,

but nothing for the additional 15 minutes. I feel that my employers were selfish for staying open the extra 45 minutes, paying an extra 30 minutes at regular rather than extra pay, and totally ignoring the additional 15 minutes. . .

Theoretically, we might expect selfishness to be less prevalent in primary than in secondary relationships. In the former the self-seeker, given the closeness of the relationship, is likely to experience social disapproval for his improprieties. Social disapproval of those who take advantage of others in everyday life, in violation of the common norms of fairness, is said to be a cost to them, which discourages such behaviour (Blau, 1964:167). Nonetheless, because selfishness rests on such human foibles as inadequate role-taking ability, a distorted sense of fairness, or a disregard or dislike for the victim, it is common in primary relations as well. There is a degree of truth to George Bernard Shaw's maxim: 'the golden rule is that there is no golden rule.'

Additionally, the person who has the least interest in the continuation of the relationship possesses the greater power in it (Ross, 1921:136; Waller and Hill, 1951: 190-2; Homans, 1974: 73-4). It is therefore possible that such persons, if so inclined, could act selfishly toward their partners more often and more exploitatively than their partners could toward them. As pointed out earlier, however, such behaviour is likely to be considered justifiable selfishness by the self-seeker. Unfortunately, the cases upon which this paper is based offer little of the kind of detail needed to shed further light on the workings of the principle of least interest in selfishness.

How then do victims cope with the more powerful self-seeker when open confrontation is too risky? When confrontation could result in loss of such significant values as affection or employment? One response available to many victims is to show their displeasure with the self-seeker's behaviour, but avoid making the direct imputation of selfishness. For instance, they might complain, whine, sulk, or joke sarcastically. Others seem to accept stoically the entire transaction on the belief that this is the natural order of things or one's lot in life. Perhaps such people think little of themselves in comparison with the dominant self-seeker. When selfish behaviour is institutionalized, as it is in some marriages, total institutions, and places of work, victims may understand their own expoitation as the price of seeking certain goals, accepting certain arrangements, or running afoul of the reigning community values. For some of these individuals there are rewards that offset the costs of selfishness.

Character

Another question of interest in the social psychology of selfishness is whether this imputation is meant to describe the situated behaviour of an individual or an aspect of his character. Everyday usage exhibits both elements: acts are selfish and the personalities who perpetrate them may be selfish too.

Gardner Murphy's (1954:624) summary of three prevailing views of selfishness indicates that philosophic and scientific thinkers on this issue have yet to reach agreement. Thomas Hobbes' position was that people are fundamentally selfish, but this orientation is controlled by the social need to accept a sovereign who in turn controls selfish behaviour. A second view, prevalent in Marxist and Christian thought, is that infant human beings are ready to be molded in any direction; they may develop a group-centred or self-centred orientation. The third view is that of John Stuart Mill, which is that people can identify with their groups and actually derive joy in and through the joy of others. Self-sacrifice and altruism, as defined by Branden, are the sorts of behaviour Mill had in mind.

The Marxist-Christian view is the most consistent with modern social psychological theory and Murphy's (1954: 624-5) own position. He holds that selfishness is learned in early childhood with the establishment of the self, and then gradually unlearned to a greater or lesser extent with socialization and approaching maturity. In a tiny minority of people learning not to be selfish continues to an exceptional level. In Kohlberg's (1968:26) moral development framework, they have reached 'stage six.' Here they are oriented by such abstract and universal moral principles as justice, reciprocity and equality of human rights, and respect for the dignity of human beings as individual persons.

But, while a few people unlearn their initial selfishness to an uncommon degree, a few others fail conspicuously to lose this childhood orientation. Several cases revolved around self-centred individuals, known in their family or friendship circles for this personal characteristic:

> My brother is a person who is constantly selfish. When he displays his selfishness, I am usually the indirect victim while my parents are hurt directly. About a month ago he decided that he wanted some things. At all costs he was determined to get them. He became sick of school and decided to quit and later go to a different school. He also wanted to buy a truck, but he had no money and no job. He had a particular truck in mind. When my dad tried to compromise by looking at less expensive trucks, he wouldn't do it. He fought constantly with my mother, father, and me. He began skipping school and getting into arguments with his teachers when

he was there. He repeatedly told the three of us how much he hated us and didn't want to be around us. He refused to help around the house in any way. He was impossible to reason with. He knew that if he kept this up long enough he would get what he wanted. He had done this same thing to a lesser degree before. My brother did quit school and my parents did countersign a loan so he could get his truck.

Conclusions

It is an ingrained rule of etiquette in our society that we refrain from the exploitative unfairness of selfishness. Most of us try to guide our actions by this rule and we expect others to do the same (though a few respondents retrospectively defined a particular act of their own as selfish). In everyday life, however, its violation becomes problematic; what victims consider selfish may fail to stand up to the justifications that self-seekers muster in support of their questionable behaviour. In the end, the question of whether we are exploited or exploitative turns on our defintion of the situation in which the allegedly self-centred act occured. And others on the scene (victim, self-seeker, bystanders) may disagree with the imputation or the attempted neutralization of it. A confrontation may follow.

All this suggests that a clear and simple rule of etiquette, such as 'avoid selfishness,' is quickly muddled when applied in daily living, where human motivation and sentiment always have an element of uncertainty and mystery.

Endnotes

1. Though I never found selfishness explicitly mentioned in the etiquette literature, it can be concluded from two sources that it is definitely bad form. Both Post (1975: 922–30) and Vanderbilt (1963: 509–19) offer advice on how to get along with others in the family. They urge us to be considerate of others's needs and interests, to try to understand their points of view, and the like. As a violation of our code of etiquette, however, selfishness is clearly more serious than, for example, slurping one's soup. Indeed, some scholars might be inclined to classify it as a violation of our moral code instead of our code of etiquette. Yet, while the effects of selfishness do vary widely in their seriousness, such behavour is infre-quently treated in the philosophical literature on ethics and then only briefly.

2. This discussion of selfishness as a violation of our code of etiquette reflects present-day custom. The future might bring a radically new

outlook on the matter, depending on how we continue to regard personal goal seeking when done at the expense of others.

3. The students were asked to describe on paper one or two acts of adult selfishness, where they were the victim and where they were accused of being self-seekers. They were instructed to use their own definitions of selfishness, which could only come from their commonsense experience.

4. The definition of the situation is the meaning individuals ascribe to their immediate present. Further theoretical treatment of this concept is available elsewhere (Stebbins, 1975b: chaps. 1–2).

5. A few respondents said they started a confrontation with their potential victims to ensure they understood the reasons behind an act (projected or executed) that might be defined as selfish. Obviously, naively selfish individuals, in their situational ignorance (Stryker, 1957; Stebbins, 1975a), would feel no need to take such initiative.

6. In the mutual form, the imputation of selfishness is one subjective or attitudinal reaction to what is known, at the organizational or structural level of analysis, as role conflict.

References

Blau, Peter M.
    1964   Exchange and Power in Social Life. New York: John Wiley.

Branden, Nathaniel
    1961   'Isn't everyone selfish?' Pp. 57-60 in Ayn Rand (ed.), The Virtue of Selfishness. New York: New American Library.

Clanton, Gordon and Lynn G. Smith (eds.)
    1977   Jealousy. Englewood Cliffs, New Jersey: Prentice-Hall.

Cooley, Charles H.
    1922   Human Nature and the Social Order (Rev. ed.). New York: Charles Scribner's Sons.

Downie, R.S. and Elizabeth Telfer
    1969   Respect for Persons. London: George Allen & Unwin.

Goffman, Erving
　　1963　Behavior in Public Places. New York: Free Press. 1967 Interaction Ritual. Chicago: Aldine

Hockart, A. M.
　　1931　'Etiquette.' Pp. 615-17 in Edwin R.A. Seligman and Alvin Johnson (eds.), Encyclopedia of the Social Sciences (Vol. 5). New York: Macmillan Co.

Homans, George C.
　　1974　Social Behavior: Its Elementary Forms (Rev. ed.). New York: Harcourt, Brace, Jovanovich.

Kohlberg, Lawrence
　　1968　'The child as a moral philosopher.' Psychology Today 2:25-30.

Lofland, Lynn H.
　　1973　A World of Strangers. New York: Basic Books.

Lyman, Stanford M. and Marvin B Scott
　　1970　A Sociology of the Absurd. New York: Appleton-Century-Crofts.

Martin, Wilfred B. W.
　　1976　The Negotiated Order of the School. Toronto: Macmillan of Canada.

Murphy, Gardner
　　1954　'Social motivation.' Pp. 601-33 in Gardner Lindzey (ed.), Handbook of Social Psychology (Vol.II). Reading, Mass.: Addison-Wesley.

Parsons, Talcott
　　1940　'Motivation of economic activities.' Canadian Journal of Economics and Political Science 6:187-203.

Post, Elizabeth L.
　　1975　The New Emily Post Etiquette. New York: Funk & Wagnalls.

Rand, Ayn
　　1961　The Virtue of Selfishness. New York: New American Library.

Ross, Edward A.
    1921 Principles of Sociology. New York: Century.

Schwartz, Barry
    1968 'The social psychology of privacy.' American Journal of Sociology 73:741-52.

Stebbins, Robert A.
    1972 'Modesty, pride, and conceit: variations in the expression of self-esteem.' Pacific Sociological Review 15:461-81.
    1975a 'Situational ignorance and its consequences.' Humboldt Journal of Social Relations 3:13-18.
    1975b Teachers and Meaning: Definitions of Classroom Situations. Leiden, Holland: E.J. Brill.
    1976 'Conceited talk; a test of hypotheses.' Psychological Reports 29:1111-16.

Stryker, Sheldon
    1957 'Role-taking accuracy and adjustment.' Sociometry 20:286-96.

Vanderbilt, Amy
    1963 Amy Vanderbilt's New Complete Book of Etiquette. Garden City, New York: Doubleday.

Waller, Willard and Reuben Hill
    1951 The Family (Rev. ed.). New York: Holt, Rinehart and Winston.

Chapter 5

SITUATIONAL IGNORANCE

For the credit of virtue it must be admitted that the greatest evils which befall mankind are caused by their crimes (La Rochefoucauld).

The greatest griefs are those we cause ourselves (Sophocles).

[from a supermarket newsletter]. *Question*: It would be helpful if price stickers were not stuck on items which have directions (e.g., recipes) on them. Often, when the sticker is removed, so is part of the directions! *Answer*: Your point is well taken. We are instructing our clerks to use some other portion of the package for pricing stickers.

Since the initial statement by Moore and Tumin (1949), a handful of sociologists have addressed themselves, in various ways, to the subject of the social functions of ignorance. The major generalization to emerge from this sprinkling of theoretical and empirical assessments is that whatever its general dysfunctions, ignorance can also have positive consequences for the ignorant person, for certain others, or for the social system. In fact, we have begun to expand our scientific understanding of an enduring theme of popular culture, which appears in such phrases as "ignorance is bliss" and "what you don't know can't hurt you" and in the decades-old Tin Pan Alley hit "It Pays to Be Ignorant."

The definition of ignorance used here is identical to that of Moore and Tumin (1949:788): "Ignorance is to be taken here as simply referring to 'not knowing,' that is, the absence of empirically valid knowledge. . . . Ignorance is to be kept distinct from 'error,' whether of fact or of logic, and from the act of *ignoring* what is known." Examination of the literature that deals explicitly with ignorance and some of that that deals implicitly with it reveals three distinct themes. First, ignorance is of two types: institutional and situational. Second, the knowledge of which we are ignorant is, to use Cooley's distinction, either material or social. Third, the consequences of ignorance may be either beneficial or unbeneficial for society or individual. To wit, they may be functional or dysfunctional at the societal level and adjustive or maladjustive at the individual level.

(1) Several years after the appearance of Moore and Tumin's paper, Schneider (1962) coined the distinction between "institutional" and "situational" ignorance. In the former the institutional and other macrosociological benefits of ignorance are traced, while in the latter its benefits are examined with reference to the immediate social situation or small network of persons or both. Schneider, as well as Moore and Tumin, were concerned primarily with institutional ignorance, relegating situational ignorance to a residual role. Perhaps for this reason we knew more, until recently, about the institutional than about the situational variety, especially when the empirical aplications of Clark (1960:575-576) and Banton (1965:48-49, 56) are recognized.

Contributions to our understanding of situational ignorance have been made by Davis (1960), Stryker (1957), Glaser and Strauss (1965:31), and Stebbins (1975:189-200). Davis studied the uncertainty of medical prognosis and the positive functions of medical ignorance for both doctors and families of poliomyelitis patients. Stryker's investigation of adjustments of parents to discrepant attitudes held by their adult children illustrates the benefits of ignorance of these attitudes by suggesting that those parents who are thus ignorant adjust better to their offspring. While most terminal patients appear to want the opposite, Glaser and Strauss point out that some wish to remain in "blissful ignorance" about their impending death. Stebbins notes that the object of a put-on, though he still suffers in other ways, benefits from being ignorant of the deceit because, at least, he experiences no embarrassment.

(2) Consideration of these observations bearing on situational and institutional ignorance, plus those reported later in this paper, indicate that, at least for situational ignorance, a distinction between types of knowledge about which we may be ignorant would also be valuable. A typology that fits the data from past research and from the present study is available in the works of Cooley (1926) and Simmel (1950:308-309). Cooley's distinction is clearest. He speaks of "spatial" or "material" knowledge, which develops from sense contacts with things and which includes its refinement into mensu-

rative science (e.g., Davis's medical uncertainty). "Personal" or "social" knowledge, on the other hand, emerges through role taking and includes an awareness of other people's thoughts, needs, sentiments, and aims that bear on the interactive situation (e.g., Stryker's parental ignorance of offsprings' attitudes). As Table 1 demonstrates, sociological knowledge of the social functions and dysfunctions of ignorance is weakest with respect to situational ignorance of social kowledge.

Table 1.
Distribution of Past Research by Types of Ignorance and Types of Knowledge

	Types of Knowledge	
Types of ignorance	Ignorance of material knowledge	Ignorance of social knowledge
Institutional	Moore & Tumin (1949) Schneider (1962) Clark (1960) Banton (1965)	(no relationship)
Situational	Davis (1960) Glaser & Strauss (1965) Stebbins (1975)	Stryker (1957)

(3) The distinction between material and social knowledge formally suggests a new line of inquiry concerning the social functions of ignorance. The ignorance considered by Moore and Tumin, Schneider, Clark, Banton, Davis, Glaser and Strauss, and Stebbins is the absence of material knowledge. The advantages of such ignorance for person or system lie in the ignorance itself ("what you don't know can't hurt you"). While ignorance of social knowledge of others in an interactive situation may also be directly beneficial in this fashion, there is a new dimension added by dint of being in contact (direct or indirect) with other people. That is, when we are ignorant of other people's aims, sentiments, needs, and the like, we may, in some way, hurt or annoy them. For such treatment, they may retaliate. Thus, our ignorance of social knowledge of others present may also indirectly serve us, and it may serve us well *or* ill. When it is advantageous, it is because those others are either unable or have chosen not to treat

us ill somehow for our thoughtlessness. It is that others fail to make life more uncomfortable or uneasy for us that makes our ignorance functional, rather than the ignorance itself.

Stryker (1957:296) in particular has noted the need for additional exploration of the ignorance of social knowledge:

> The assertion that knowledge is necessarily adjustive cannot be defended; it is highly probably that the unqualified assertion that ignorance is adjustive is equally invalid. The problem, now, is to specify further the conditions under which knowledge or ignorance is adjustive or maladjustive.

Indeed, Simmel (1955:19) suggests two reasons why ignorance of social knowledge is frequently maladjustive:

> If we did not even have the power and the right to rebel against tyranny, arbitrariness, moodiness, tactlessness, we could not bear to have any relation to people from whose characters we thus suffer. We would feel pushed to take desperate steps. . . . Not only because of the fact. . .that oppression usually increases if it is suffered calmly and without protest, but also because opposition gives us inner satisfaction, distraction, relief. . . . Our opposition makes us feel that we are not completely victims of the circumstances. It allows us to prove our strength consciously. . . .

There are events in our lives that offer an excellent opportunity to explore further some of the conditions under which the lack of social knowledge is adjustive and maladjustive. They are the *nettlesome encounters* we have with our fellowman, which are experienced while engaging in the routine activities of everyday life. They are the subject of this paper.

Nettlesome Encounters

Nettlesome encounters may be defined as those interactions among people characterized, in whole or in part, by **heedless aggression** by one or more others. Aggression is here defined as "the delivery of noxious stimuli to another organism" (Buss, 1963:1).[1] It is heedless when it stems from the aggressor's inattentiveness of failure to see, observe, or take note of others' salient thoughts, sentiments, needs, and aims. He lacks social knowledge, at least momentarily, of those against whom he has aggressed.

Heedless aggression can be best understood by contrasting it with two common forms of situated aggression which presuppose some degree of social knowledge of the target person.[2] Throughout the remainder of the discussion Person A is the initiator or initiators of aggression toward another person or group of persons, called Person B. That is, Person A delivers the first noxious stimulus in the interaction between him and B.

In what could be called **vexatious aggression**, noxious acts are purposely aimed by Person A at B because certain of his beliefs, attitudes, or behaviors annoy A. Social knowledge of B is needed to a degree sufficient for an effective attack on him.[3] Vexatious aggression is exemplified by teen-age boys hazing an adult homosexual, townsmen perpetrating a practical joke on the village fool, children taunting a deformed classmate, or motorists honking furiously at other motorists whose driving has upset them. Aggression, here, is normally an expression of a desire to amuse oneself, to vent one's irritation, to remove a frustrating impediment to the achievement of a goal, to retaliate for some small injustice, or to do a combination of these.

Frustration-avoidance aggression results from Person A's conscious enactment of a noxious act or acts while pursing some goal. Again, A has enough social knowledge of B to know he will be upset by his behavior. Person A wants to reach his goal and cares little about how he irritates B in the course of doing so. In frustration-avoidance aggression A is seeking to avert potential frustration, rather than responding to an existing state of it, as in some vexatious aggression. It is all too often seen in the behavior of the apartment-dwelling individuals who turn up the volume on their television sets or phonographs, even though they know their neighbors object.

One might argue that seeking to avoid imminent frustration is the same, psychologically, as reacting to its actual presence. However, reacting to potential frustration with aggression means the aggressor must justify to himself, on grounds other than annoyance, his role as initiator of aggression in that particular interactive situation. Moreover, his reactive behavior is likely to be different from that motivated by feelings of irritation and possibly the wish to retaliate as caused by existing frustration.

Two incidents illustrate the phenomenon of the nettlesome encounter and the part played in it by heedless aggression by A against B.

Incident I

I was driving home late one August afternoon along an artery that carries rush hour traffice to the suburbs of a large city. Suddenly, a motorist in the right lane (Motorist Number 1), apparently realizing he had to be in the left lane in order to exit from the highway a short distance away, swung recklessly into that lane, causing another motorist (Motorist Number 2) to brake sharply. The reaction of Motorist 2 was spontaneous. He swerved from the left lane into the vacant space in the right lane left by Motorist 1, passed him, cut into a small opening ahead of him, and somehow managed to stop for the traffic signal, which had just changed to red. Number 1's tires screeched as he fought to avoid a collision with the rear of 2's car.

Incident 2

Recently, students living in one of the residences of a large and prestigious eastern university in the United States were told they could no longer keep such animals as dogs and cats there. The reason given by the master was that the students were disobeying the rules by allowing their pets to urinate and defecate within the building. The janitors, said the master took a dim view of this practice.

Conditions of Heedless Aggression

Like most other people, I had been going through life experiencing the needless aggression of others and occasionally perpetrating my own on them without ever identifying such human actions as special. This identification, once made, brought it to the level of awareness, where it became possible to collect descriptions of instances of it from my daily experience and that of my friends and acquaintances. Accounts of others' heedless aggression, where they are conscious of it, are relatively easy to gather. People often seem to enjoy discussing their minor clashes with their fellowman. For they see their behavior as justified in light of the circumstances, and relating it is possibly good catharsis as well as good conversation.

Over approximately four years, fifty-seven instances of heedless aggression were collected in this fashion, many of which occurred in a city of approximately one hundred thousand people. This is hardly an adequate procedure for establishing the precise frequency with which such aggression occurs in the various situations of everyday life. It does, however, produce a sufficient base of empirical data for generating grounded theory about this subject. That is, enough instances were observed or described to me by others to define this phenomenon and to link it with four circumstances in which it normally appears.[4]

First, nettlesome encounters appear to be characteristically urban, because they occur most commonly, though not exclusively, in impersonal settings. That is, Person A generally treats Person B as a nonperson. In these settings it is less a matter of inaccurate role taking as considered, for instance, by Stryker (1962), than a matter of no role taking at all. It should be noted, though, that some of Stryker s findings appear to be related to this proposition. For example, he found role-taking accuracy increases between people having frequent contact. When nettlesome encounters are more personal there is usually a momentary lapse in the role taking process, which leads to heedless aggression by A.

Second, within these impersonal, urban settings, heedless aggression is enacted while engaging in routine activities or the activities of everyday life. Third, this aggression, though it may have far-reaching consequences, begins as part of a relatively trivial or superficial act. To illustrate, in Incident I, Motorist 1 was probably driving home from work (routine activity) and casually decided to change lanes on the highway (trivial act). In other words, the lane changing act was presumably carried out with only minimal thought given to its actual execution and none to its consequences.

Fourth, heedless aggression often takes place while we are preoccupied, while we are so lost in thought about a problem or an event, big or small, that we become oblivious to the situational requirements of others. Such preoccupation occurs within the context of routine behavior, as when we inadvertently collide with another person while looking for an item in a large store or fail to signal our intention to turn left while driving because we are engrossed in a radio program.

Ignorance or lack of social knowledge of others in nettlesome encounters is adjustive (functional, in systems terminology) when Person A is able to pursue his immediate, or within-the-situation, aims without hindrance or annoyance, even though he has aggressed against B in the process. That is, ignorance is adjustive at least for the moment, for unpleasant ramifications of the encounter beyond the immediate situation could call such a judgment into question. On the other hand, such ignorance is maladjustive (dysfunctional) when A is either hindered or annoyed or both by B's reaction to his unwitting aggression. In other words, B reciprocates with some form of aggression against A.

Let us turn now to some of the conditions found in impersonal settings in which social knowledge is frequently absent and in which social knowledge is frequently absent in which this absence may be maladjustive or adjustive. In the following section the conditions under which ignorance is maladjustive or adjustive are examined with reference to personal settings.

Impersonal Settings

Three settings are considered: driving, pedestrian, and occupational. Here, face-to-face contact, if there is any, is brief or highly formal or both.

1) Examples of **heedless aggression in driving** behavior are legion. I have observed people park their cars directly in front of the only sidewalk leading to the entrance of a building, forcing others who wish to enter the building to climb over snowdrifts in the winter or walk across the lawn in the summer. At least in some parts of North America, drivers of delivery vans, service trucks, and even automobiles, when engaged in some activity at private homes, frequently park their vehicles in or in front of the driveways to those homes. If he is travelling by car, the occupant is either hemmed in or barred from entering his premises.

There are other common incidents in driving that anyone with any experience in this activity will immediately recognize as annoying. Double-parked vehicles, especially when they slow our progress, get our dander up. So do motorists who pull onto the road in front of us, force us to slow down abruptly, and then proceed at a leisurely pace. Failure to signal one's intention to turn can provoke anger in motorists nearby.

These types of incidents generate in Person B a desire to return the aggression, though this depends on finding the opportunity to do so. Driving a car is, by and large, an impersonal activity. So, we honk angrily at other drivers who nettle us, pass them and cut back in on them, tailgate them, reprove them, and, rarely, get out of our car and punch them in the nose. A colleague of mine once gained experience as the object of reciprocated aggression for his own heedless aggression when he obliviously parked his car in a private parking space on campus. When he returned, he found his vehicle surrounded by others. He had to wait until a lengthy meeting ended before the cars were moved. When offended drivers have a chance to reciprocate thus, situational ignorance of the sort considered here is maladjustive.

At times, however, there is no opportunity to retaliate or vent one's anger or frustration, and, therefore, ignorance has worked to A's advantage. Perhaps A passes the offended driver going in the opposite direction or he is inside a building where our honking at his double-parked car cannot be heard. Under such conditions, we, as Person B, are unable to upset A for his thoughtlessness or hinder his progress toward his goal.

2) **Heedless aggression by pedestrians** is also prevalent. Included in this category are all activities, within the situational limits already set out, that people do on foot. Again, examples are easy to find: two women

unthinkingly blocking a supermarket aisle while having a chat, a group of students clogging a hall as they converse, a person ambling across the street in front of a moving vehicle, or people stepping in front of others as all try to watch a parade. Blocking passageways is one typical way human beings encourage nettlesome encounters with others. Take, for example, those who stop just inside the entrance to a terminal after leaving an airplane, or stop just inside a doorway of a room that many others are trying to enter or leave. Finally, as Incident II illustrates, people may engender such encounters by failing to curb their pets or take them from the building when they eliminate.[5]

Here, as in driving, an absence of social knowledge by Person A can be maladjustive for him. Those who heedlessly block passageways may get shoved, bumped, or even spoken to harshly. Those who saunter in front of a motorist who is in a hurry may get honked at or come uncomfortably close to getting run down. Person B would generally seem to have a better opportunity for reciprocal aggression in pedestrian nettlesome encounters than in those of driving, simply because Person A is usually close by. But, such proximity is no guarantee B will act thus. Since there is a tendency in our society to avoid open face-to-face clashes, ignorance is perhaps less likely to be maladjustive here than in driving situations. Still, Wolff (1973:40) found that when the experimenter intentionally bumped into a pedstrian in New York City, angry staring and abusive remarks commonly followed. He goes on to note:

> Knowledge of, and competence in, monitoring and negotiating behavior, body control, and positioning patterns are the taken-for-granted parts of every pedestrian's repertoire, and failures in any of the above behaviors that result in intrusions or array disruptions may quickly be attributed to a lack of effort or concern, eliciting complaints or challenges (1973:48).

3) **Occupational heedless aggression** refers to acts of this sort committed during the course of earning one's livelihood, and excludes driving and pedestrian acts carried out in this connection. Store clerks, for instance, may inadvertently place the price tag of a product over information printed on the package or the product itself. Occasionally, the information obscured is needed by the customer to help him decide whether or not to buy the item; he may need to know how to assemble it, how large it is, or how much of it there is. This short-sightedness irritates customers who may attempt to peel off the tag or who root through the merchandise in search of one more favorably placed. This results in the display of merchandise being disarrayed or the price tag and even the package being damaged. And, the clerk, owing to this lack of empathy for

the customer, must now rearrange the merchandise or replace the tag. Moreover, he, and store personnel in general, may be further disadvanted, as a result of their ignorance, when the customer sets about venting his irritation. For the customer, now in a cantankerous mood from the price tag episode, may throw wastepaper on the floor instead of using the available trash receptacles or take a shopping cart from the store and leave it in the parking lot.

Official notices from educational, government, and business organizations sometimes turn into forms of heedless aggression when their authors accidentally omit information important to the reader or otherwise fail to take account of people's needs. Here, the receiver (Person B) is treated as a person - unlike most heedless aggression in impersonal settings - but there is a momentary lapse in role taking by the sender of the message (Person A). Verbal statements made to patients by physicians and to clients by lawyers or social workers may contain similar defects. In England, outside a park in the Cornish resort of New Quay, the town council put up a notice saying "no person shall walk, run, stand, sit, or lie on the grass in this pleasure ground" (*Dallas Morning News*, 1974). In such situations, reciprocated aggression is unlikely for A, however, because B usually finds it awkward or virtually impossible to express his anger in a way that upsets A. A's heedless aggression is therefore adjustive for him, at least for the moment.

Personal Settings

The observations and accounts on which this paper is based suggest that heedless aggression is significantly less frequent in personal than in impersonal settings. No wonder. There is usually more frequent contact between individuals in personal settings. As noted earlier, role-taking accuracy increases with increasing contact. It also tends to increase with the significance of the role area for the relationship and with the significance of the other person for the role taker (Stryker, 1962). Additionally, since interpersonal relationships are, by definition, closer in personal settings, it is reasonable to conclude that social knowledge of Person B is valued for its use in maintaining the bond. Therefore, the very desire to role take is stronger than it normally is in impersonal circumstances (c.f., Lauer and Boardman, 1971:146).

Less heedless aggression, in itself, means less reciprocated aggression. But, even if heedless aggression were frequent in personal settings, it is likely that reciprocation of it would be less frequent than in impersonal settings. For, in most personal settings, contact between Persons A and B is more enduring. Hence, the tendency to avoid face-to-face friction is joined by the desire to avoid spending much time near an individual one has just attacked. If nothing else, prolonged contact gives the victim a better chance for reprisal.

All this considered, several instances of heedless aggression were observed or described as taking place in personal settings. Occasionally, we do fail to take the role of the other. Indeed, this probably occurs in nearly every kind of personal setting. Four are examined here: domestic, conversational, vicinal, and leisured.

1) **Domestic heedless aggression** refers to such acts perpetrated by Person A in Person B's home. There are at least two sets of physical conditions which, if unfavorably altered by A, are likely to irritate B. The first is that B's home is an establishment whose appearance in terms of neatness, cleanliness, decoration, and similar considerations communicates, to all who enter, B's standards and abilities along these lines. The second is that, because B spends a good deal of time there, his home must be livable; to wit, it must, for him, be healthy, feel comfortable, smell pleasant, sound good, look attractive, and the like.

Examples of domestic heedless aggression abound. One is the mother who, accompanied by her child who has a bad cold, visits a friend's home, thereby exposing the friend's children to the infection. Another is that of the careless cigarette smoker who, by inadvertently dropping ashes on the living room carpet, burns a hole in it. A third is the serviceman who absentmindedly tracks mud into the kitchen in the course of fixing the dishwasher. The cigar smoker, by polluting the domestic atmosphere, exemplifies heedless aggression, especially from the hostess's viewpoint.

Each of these incidents unwittingly nettles someone in the home, usually the homemaker. But, for reasons just stated, they are unlikely to lead to reciprocated aggression.

2) **Conversational heedless aggression** can occur in homes as elsewhere, but it is not considered domestic because its effects appear to be the same whether inside or outside the homes of those affected. There is nothing special about such conversational aggression when enacted in someones' home. Numerous inadvertent conversational acts by Person A may irritate B: blowing cigarette smoke in his face, talking so softly that he is unable to hear what is said, or changing abruptly a subject of conversation he is intensely interested in. Many people are annoyed, even angered, at the vaunted conversationalist who, with talk about his achievements, monopolizes the interaction in such a way that no one can talk about their own achievements or interests (Stebbins, 1972). Discourse of this sort

may be defined by the listeners as a noxious intrusion into an otherwise sociable conversation as well as a violation of conversational etiquette. The conceited speaker, however, is unaware that his statements are interpreted thus. As in domestic nonempathy, conversational nonempathy is inconsequential, and therefore, adjustive; it seems to generate little or no reciprocated aggression.

3) **Vicinal heedless aggression** refers to the absence of social knowledge in Person B's neighbors (Person A) in an apartment building or in a single-dwelling neighborhood. Ignorant acts are common here, although they are sometimes difficult to distinguish from frustration-avoidance and vexatious aggression. There is, for example, the man next door who lets his dog bark through the night, the couple above who has raucous parties, the homeowner down the street whose house and yard resemble a rural slum, and the energetic neighbor whose power mower awakens us at eight o'clock Sunday mornings.

Lack of social knowledge by A in this type of setting can lead to reciprocated aggression by B, which is maladjustive for A. If the couple above holds loud gatherings that run far into the night and that disturb those living below, the latter may make a special effort to produce noise in the morning when the former are trying to sleep. Neighborhood dogs that persist in barking much of the night have been known to get poisoned, much to their masters' horror. When B is not inclined to retaliate directly, he may adopt an I-don't-care orientation toward A. Whatever assistance A might appreciate receiving from B (e.g., loan of a ladder, push for his stalled car), B tries to avoid giving, saying, in effect, "why should I make an extra effort to help him, when he treats me badly?"

4) Finally, **heedless aggression**, which is usually adjustive for A, occurs **in leisured settings**. We get upset with people who talk loudly to each other throughout a play, concert, motion picture, or speech. Even worse is the person who persists in talking to us under these circumstances. Likewise, we may become irritated with someone who stands up in front of us in order to see better a crucial play in football. This sort of momentary ignorance of others' needs, despite the mass setting, is personal so far as B is concerned, because he must coexist in proximity with A for the duration of the performance, game, movie, or other event and because he would have to confront A directly in order to express his anger toward him. Thus, aggression is unlikely to be reciprocated.

Summary and Conclusions

Situational ignorance is sometimes adjustive and sometimes maladjustive in the many nettlesome encounters of everyday life in which we heedlessly aggress against others. Observational data have shown that there are at least four circumstances in which heedless aggression and the ignorance of social knowledge typically appear: in impersonal, urban settings in which others are treated as nonpersons or with a momentary absence of role taking; in routine activities; as part of a relatively trivial act; while preoccupied.

There are a number of conditions under which the absence of ignorance of social knowledge is maladjustive in nettlesome encounters. Aggression is especially likely to be reciprocated by Person B, and is therefore maladjustive, in the impersonal setting of driving, though this depends on B finding an opportunity to return the aggression. In pedestrian and occupational settings such reciprocation is less likely, only because face-to-face and status relations, being more common there, militate against this desire. In personal settings ignorance of social knowledge tends to be maladjustive only in vicinal situations.

Obversely, this ignorance is adjustive, even in impersonal driving settings, when Person B is unable to retaliate for A's heedlessness. The face-to-face and status relations of pedestrian and occupational settings also contribute to the adjustive possibilities of a lack of social knowledge. Similarly, face-to-face circumstances discourage aggressive reciprocation by B in domestic, conversational, and leisured personal settings.

Clearly, broader and, at the same time, more controlled study is needed of the social functions and dysfunctions of ignorance. Inquiry into the functions of the ignorance of social knowledge, as contrasted with the ignorance of material knowledge, will proceed differently. It is preeminently a social psychological problem, while ignorance of material knowledge, though by no means devoid of social psychological implications, has been treated from a structural-institutional perspective up to this point. By adding the dimension of the aggressive reactions of others to the consideration of the social functions of ignorance, new possibilities emerge for theory and research in this area.

Endnotes

I.   Though this is a broader definition than that employed by some psychologists, its breadth makes it particularly useful in the study of routine interaction (e.g., Doob and Gross, 1968).

2.   No claim is made here that this classification includes all types of aggression possible in social situations. Its only purpose is to clarify the role of heedless aggression in nettlesome encounters by showing what it is not.

3. This is a relatively superficial degree of social knowledge. A high degree of such knowledge would probably lead A, in many instances, to avoid attacking B.

4.   More systematic field study of the subject of heedless aggression would be difficult. Apart from the fact that it is unwitting behavior for Person A is the further observation that Person B experiences it only occasionally. The observer would have to spend hours, perhaps days, in some settings in order to see even one instance of it. Then he might find, as with automobile drivers and people attending a film, that he would be unable to interview either party in the encounter about their lack of social knowledge or their irritation. Like role distance behavior (see Stebbins, 1969:409), the study of this form of ignorance and its consequences is better pursued as part of a larger investigation of some other phenomenon.

5.   Some of the time this sort of behavior of Person A may be interpreted as frustration-avoidance aggression rather than heedless aggression.

References

Banton, Michael
1965 ROLES. London: Tavistock.

Buss, Arnold H.
1963 "Physical aggression in relation to different frustrations."
JOURNAL OF ABNORMAL AND SOCIAL PSYCHOL-
OGY 67(1):1- 7.

Clark, Burton R.
1960 "The cooling-out function in higher education." AMERICAN
JOURNAL OF SOCIOLOGY 32 (July):59-79.

DALLAS MORNING NEWS
1974 (Tuesday, November 12):3A.

Davis, Fred
1960 "Uncertainty in medical prognosis, clinical and function."
AMERICAN JOURNAL OF SOCIOLOGY 66 (July):41-47.

Doob, Anthony V. and Alan E. Gross
1968 "Status of frustrator as an inhibitor of horn-honking responses."
JOURNAL OF SOCIAL PSYCHOLOGY 76:213- 218.

Glaser, Barney G. and Anselm L. Strauss
1965 AWARENESS OF DYING. Chicago: Aldine.

Lauer, Robert H. and Linda Boardman
1971 "Role taking: theory, typology, and propositions." SOCIOL-
OGY AND SOCIAL RESEARCH 55 (January):137-148.

Moore, Wilbert E. and Melvin M. Tumin
1949 "Some social functions of ignorance." AMERICAN SOCIO-
LOGICAL REVIEW 14 (December):787-795.

Schneider, Louis
1962 "The role of ignorance in sociological theory." AMERICAN
SOCIOLOGICAL REVIEW 27 (August):492- 508.

Simmel, Georg
  1950 THE SOCIOLOGY OF GEORG SIMMEL. Trans. Kurt Wolff, New York:Free Press.
  1955 CONFLICT AND THE WEB OF GROUP- AFFILIATIONS. Trans. Kurt Wolff and Reinhard Bendix. New York:Free Press.

Stebbins, Robert A.
  1969 "Role distance, role-distance behavior, and jazz musicians." BRITISH JOURNAL OF SOCIOLOGY 20 (December)406-415.
  1972 "Modesty, pride, and conceit: variations in the expression of self- esteem." PACIFIC SOCIOLOGICAL REVIEW 15 (October):461-481.
  1975 "Putting people on: deception of our fellowman in everyday life." SOCIOLOGY AND SOCIAL RESEARCH 59 (April):189-200.

Stryker, Sheldon
  1957 "Role-taking accuracy and adjustment." SOCIOMETRY 20 (December):286-296.
  1962 "Conditions of accurate role taking." Pp. 41-62 in Arnold M. Rose (ed.), HUMAN BEHAVIOR AND SOCIAL PROCESSES. Boston:Houghton Mifflin.

Wolff, Michael
  1973 "Notes on the behavior of pedestrians." Pp. 35-48 in Arnold Birenbaum and Edward Sagarin (eds.), PEOPLE IN PLACES: THE SOCIOLOGY OF THE FAMILIAR. New York:Praeger.

Chapter 6

MODESTY, PRIDE, & CONCEIT

Mark Twain, whenever feats of heroism or ingeunity were being bragged about, would come forth with a little story of his own, which usually climaxed the discussion: "There was a fire in Hannibal one night, and old man Hankinson got caught in the fourth story of the burning house. It looked as if he were a goner. None of the ladders was long enough to reach him. The crowd stared at one another, nobody could think of anything to do. Then, all of a sudden, boys, an idea occurred to me. "Fetch a rope," I yelled, "somebody fetch a rope," and with great presence of mind, I flung the end of it up to old man Hankinson; "Tie it around your waist," I yelled. The old man did so, and I pulled him down (from Edmund Fuller. *2500 Anecdotes for All Occasions.* New York: Avenel, 1970, p. 19).

Few topics in sociology and social psychology have enjoyed greater attention over longer period of time than the topic of the rise, maintenance, and loss of the attitude of self-esteem or the good opinion of oneself stemming from satisfaction with one's achievements. William James was among the first to show an interest in this aspect of human nature, and, since his day, countless scholars have contributed an impressive number of studies toward our increased understanding of it.

This paper focuses on the behavioral expression of self-esteem; an aspect of the presentation of self or the process in which a person's views of himself influence his actions in social situations. Hence, other topics in self-concept research, such as the development and maintenance of self-

AUTHOR'S NOTE: *This is an expanded version of a paper presented at the Annual Meeting of the American Sociological Association, New Orleans, August 28-31, 1972. I wish to thank Jean Briggs, Ronald Joudrey, and Robert Paine; their comments and suggestions have added much to its overall quality.*

esteem and the identification and description of its psychological correlates (for example, orientation toward others, degree of confidence,
formation of goals), are residual to the discussion. Despite persistent
concentration over the years on the broader subject of self-esteem, there
has been no systematic consideration, so far as this author is aware, of its
behavioral expression. This is not to say that there has been no research on
or discussion of such behavior, but only that the research and discussion
generally are disconnected and short on conceptual precision. Attempts at
developing a coherent statement of the behavioral expression of esteem,
which could be linked to the overall theory of self-esteem, are absent.[1]

This is unfortunate, since half the story is omitted when we speak only
of the internal attitude and fail to consider the external activity that
proceeds from it. Attitudes are incipient acts; the attitude and its behavioral
expression are actually different phases of the same process (Mead,
1934:5-13; 1938:3-25). And systematic study of the external aspects of
esteem should produce a fascinating picture, for even brief reflection
discloses that there is enormous variation in the way in which we manifest
the positive feelings we have about ourselves.

As a start toward a more comprehensive view of self-esteem, I wish to
present some hypotheses about modesty, pride, and conceit as distinct
modes of verbal behavior issuing from this attitude. However, it should be
made clear at the outset that, although discourse is one way of expressing
these three, it is not the only way. Actions alone can convey conceit, for
example, as seen in strutting military figures, swaggering athletes, and
ceremonial excess.[2] Della Casa (1958:45) believed that overdecorating
oneself with jewelry is a sign of vanity. The decision to concentrate solely
on the verbal expression of modesty, pride, and conceit is based strictly on
practicality; it is enough to tackle in a conjectural venture such as this.
After the general discussion of the nature of modesty, pride, and conceit,
certain structural and situational conditions for their variation are examined.

The Nature of Modesty, Pride, and Conceit

Perhaps because it simplifies our cognitive world, we have a tendency to
judge whole personalities as modest, proud, or conceited, as if these modes
were also traits of character. Though valid to some extent, rigid adherence
to this notion obscures two important points. In the first place, modest,
proud, and conceited behavior is focused; it is enacted with reference to our
accomplishments in lines of activity regarded by us and certain others
present in the situation as major forms of positive self-identification.[3] For

example, as we shall see later, men may speak proudly of an accomplishment before one group of people and modestly of it before another. In the second place, some achievements, because of their obvious mediocrity, constitute an insufficient foundation on which to build self-worth; thus they fail to qualify as something to be proud of or modest about.

Moreover, a person is proud, conceited, or modest before an *audience*: those present in the situation whose opinions of his behavior there he values.[4] Clearly, there are two viewpoints from which to identify behavior as typical of one of these three modes: what the actor intends and what the audience perceives.[5] In many instances-perhaps most-actor and audience seem to agree on their identification; what the actor intends as modest discourse, for example, is perceived as such by the audience. But it is also possible, especially with conceit, that there will be occasional discrepancies between what the actor intends and what the audience perceives. Certain common discrepancies are discussed later.

The essence of each mode lies in its pointed reference to the speaker; the actor expresses his feelings about *his* accomplishments. Little can be said at this time about the origin of these feelings other than that they result from the complex interplay of judgments about his accomplishments made by himself and certain others in the same field according to specified standards. However, since these standards frequently are embodied in varying degrees in the achievements of particular persons ranging from neophytes to doyens, talk concerning personal attainment usually includes reference to the work of these people as well. That is to say, we often discuss the strengths and weaknesses of our own efforts by comparing them with those of someone else at, below, or above our level of performance. In these comparisons, the way we treat the accomplishments of these reference others is, therefore, an important aspect of behavior perceived as modest, proud, or conceited. Additionally, our achievements may be built upon or in reaction to related works carried out by others, thereby necessitating reference to them. In sum, it is reasonable to differentiate verbal modesty, pride, and conceit by amount and kind of discourse about the strengths and weaknesses of the actor's achievements and by amount and kind of discourse about the strengths and weaknesses of the related achievements of others.

Whatever the viewpoint, modesty and pride are often seen as socially acceptable variations in the expression of self-esteem. On one side, modesty is bordered by the form of humility, which is characterized by low personal regard as manifested in a debasing reference to self.[6] Pride, on the other hand, is bordered by conceit. Both conceit and the self-debasing form of humility can be considered minor forms of deviant behavior; persons who act this way are so labeled because they have violated the rules of etiquette held for those who engage in talk about self-worth. It is noteworthy that behavior identified as conceit usually is defined as such only by the audience, since most people, because of the stigma attached to this sort of talk, try to avoid boasting (at least very much) when they believe the audience will perceive their behavior this way.[7] When boasting does occur, most of these actors view their utterances as simply a form of pride. As for humility, it appears to be expressed consciously only in response to certain religious principles. Also, it is probably true that conceit and humility are most common among those who either are unaware of the community's rules for discourse about personal achievement or are unable to abide by them in an acceptable manner for whatever reason. Under these circumstances, conceit and humility are expressed unwittingly.

Achievement and Conversational Etiquette

Any treatment of modesty, pride, and conceit must begin with a consideration of the rules of etiquette that guide our talk about our achievements and their relationships to similar achievements of others. Etiquette, says Hockart (1931:615), is the body of forms of conventional decorum or manners into which one's behavior is cast. For roughly four hundred years, the Western world has been cultivating the general theory and art of manners from which the more specific rules of etiquette stem. A number of enduring principles of decorum bear directly on the conversational etiquette of achievement.[8] For example, Lord Chesterfield advised his nephew to talk often but never to dominate conversation and never to speak of himself (see Pear, 1939:34). Della Casa (1958:46-47) offered similar advice to his fellow Italians. He also counseled avoidance of vainglorious speech. Furthermore, it is indecorous to degrade ourselves in conversation, except when, as Maurois (1930:37) noted, we are with someone who already acknowledges our qualities. Emily Post (1957:45-57), though she refers to them as forms of etiquette, recommends these same principles of decorum. To these she adds that we must avoid being critical of others and express genuine appreciation for their accomplishments.

At least six rules of etiquette that guide our talk about our achievements and their relationships to similar achievements of others can be listed:

(1) We ought not to monopolize conversations with self-centered talk.

(2) When discussing the merits of our achievements, we ought to avoid overemphasizing them. That is, we are expected both to omit laudatory remarks about them and to refrain from talking about them at length.

(3) When discussing the weaknesses of our achievements, we ought to be candid. That is, we are expected to treat the weaknesses of our own achievements with the same degree of openness, impartiality, and analytic precision we use to treat the weaknesses of others' achievements.

(4) Even though we ought to be candid when discussing the weaknesses of our achievements, we also ought to refrain from general depreciation of those achievements.

(5) When comparing our own efforts with the generally recognized strengths of the achievements of others in our field (including those others whom we regard as equal or inferior to us), we ought to express approval of those strengths. That is, we ought not to speak with aloofness or belittlement, but rather we ought to speak with genuine appreciation. Likewise, we ought to avoid envious, jealous, and sour-grapes comments. Finally, approval of the strengths of the achievements of others ought to be expressed in our willingness to consider them at length in conversation.

(6) When comparing our own efforts with what we define as the weaknesses of the achievements of others in our field (including those others whom we regard as equal or inferior to us), we ought to be charitable. That is, we are expected to treat these weaknesses objectively, if not compassionately, and thus to refrain from making comparisons invidiously.

These rules are, of course, ideal statements. Actual conversational behavior varies markedly, even within the range of acceptability. This variation is apparent in the following discussion of the degree of conformity to the rules when expressing modesty, pride, and conceit.

Turning first to modest behavior, the individual who intends to act in this fashion aims for ideal or nearly ideal conformity to the rules of etiquette that pertain to discourse on the personal achievements of oneself and others.[9] In other words, he refrains from dominating the conversation with talk about his achievements. When he does display his feelings about them, he candidly discusses their weaknesses and carefully avoids over-emphasizing their merits. In fact, he may even evince embarrassment at times when speaking positively of his attainments. Consideration of his accomplishments may lead him to make comparisons with related accomplishments of others in his field, including those of his equals and inferiors. The modest-appearing person treats what he regards as the strengths of these accomplishments with approval, if not admiration. When he discusses the shortcomings of others' works, which is relatively infrequent, he is likely to do so with charity.

It is possible to distinguish modesty, whether intended by the actor or perceived by the audience, from its cousin, self-debasing humility. The modest-appearing person respects what he has achieved. For he continuously calls attention to this conviction by avoiding any depreciation of his work, by imparting a generalized sense of self-assurance, and by communicating a variety of skillfully phrased and skillfully placed remarks that suggest the extent and quality of his achievement without offending the listener. Maurois (1930:71-72) notes, for example, that self-assurance is expressed in slowness and deliberateness of speech.

Since it is unlikely that men will engage knowingly in conceit, our discussion of this mode of self-expression will be limited to the audience's perception of such behavior. Among the cues audiences use to identify discourse as conceited is the monopolization of conversation with self-centered talk. Specifically, the actor is seen as overstressing the significance of his accomplishments, while barely touching on their shortcomings. In this display, he also may contrast invidiously his accomplishments with similar accomplishments of others by dwelling too long and too harshly on the weaknesses of their efforts and too little on the generally acknowledged strengths of these efforts. In this connection, he may be especially critical of his peers and inferiors. It is possible, too, that while drawing unfavorable comparisons between his own achievements and those of his rivals, a person who manifests conceit may be forced to consider certain outstanding contributions made by them. When this occurs, he is likely to adopt what is perceived by the audience as a jealous, envious, or sour-grapes outlook, except perhaps with regard to those who are far superior. By focusing on his own achievements in this fashion, he fosters the belief that he is firmly convinced of his preeminence over all or a segment of those participating in the line of activity under consideration.[10]

Yet it is possible that for some audiences, a conceited-appearing person - except the one who does so intentionally (see note 7) - unwittingly conveys the impression that he is uncertain, perhaps exceptionally so, about the standing of his achievement in their eyes. He is uncertain how they evaluate it and where they rank it in relation to the achievements of others, while requiring greater than normal surety in such matters.[11] Still, I am not suggesting that these people actually have low regard for their achievements or that this is even a possibility; such is akin to humility. Those who behave conceitedly have a good opinion of the accomplishment in question; it is only the degree of goodness that is in doubt.

Because the actor is concerned thus, he is seen as attempting to manipulate the audience's impressions of his achievement, which may include merely bringing it to their attention. But he suffers from overmotivation to communicate information about this subject and insensitivity to or lack of respect for particular norms, for he violates the audience's expectations about how people should discuss personal achievement. Indeed, the only rule of achievement-related conversational etiquette he is certain to honor is the rule of avoidance of depreciation of his accomplishments. In other words, the person who acts conceited is poorly demeaned, whereas those who act proud or modest are more or less well demeaned (see Goffman, 1956).

The proud-appearing person, although aware of the rules pertaining to discourse about personal attainment, is seen by the audience as having a stong desire to discuss his efforts. This desire leads him at times to renounce the satisfying approval that comes with being modest or conforming ideally to these rules. Yet, his behavior falls within the margin of acceptability; he still is viewed by the audience as conforming in this respect, though his presentation of self may border, for some, on the objectionable.

Thus, we come to the question of how the audience differentiates proud behavior from that which is modest or conceited. One suggestion is that the person who behaves proudly is identified by his tendency to devote more time to the virtues of his own achievements than modesty would allow, while striving to avoid discussion of their weaknesses. In doing so, he is more inclined than those who express modesty to compare the deficiencies of the related efforts of others in his field with his own work. But in contrast to both conceit and modesty, he does so objectiely, evincing neither compassion nor scorn for the deficiencies. And he who acts proudly is seen as wishing to avoid discussion of the generally recognized strengths of the accomplishments of others as these pertain to his own accomplishments. When forced to consider these strengths, he tends to treat them with haste, perhaps even indifference. That is, he does not avoid them or treat them with belittlement to the extent done in conceit, but he does fail to weigh them at length or express genuine appreciation as characteristic of modesty. Moreover, it is possible that some proudly behaved individuals actualy appear somewhat envious or jealous of the generally applauded achievements of others.

Although, from the audience's viewpoint, it may look as if the conceited-appearing person has a more favorable opinion of himself than he who behaves modestly, from the standpoint of the sensitive observer, this is doubtful. Several observations support this view. One is Cooley's (1922:230-235): there is greater self-assurance among those who comport themselves modestly or proudly when compared with those who comport themselves conceitedly.[12] Underlying this self-assurance is the actor's realization that, according to his standards, he is progressing well in his field of endeavor. Another observation is based on the very nature of modesty; he who conforms closely to the audience's expectations is rewarded with its approbation. Finally, it is possible the actor is able to garner self-respect from the knowledge that he is being honest both with others and with himself; that he is not masquerading the significance of his accomplishment or their standing in relation to those of his fellows.

Having considered the nature of modesty, pride, and conceit, we are now ready to proceed to a treatment of the structural and situation conditions for their expression.[13] These conditions constitute a set of qualifications and further refinements to the foregoing discussion.

Structural Conditions

There are two perspectives from which to tackle the matter of the structural conditions influencing the expression of conceit and pride: the actor's position or social identity within the line of activity under consideration and the positions or social identities of those in the audience as perceived by the actor. The actor's location is best approached from the standpoint of career. And, since the expression of self-esteem is a personal matter, our principal focus will be the "subjective career," or the actor's recognition and interpretation of past and future events associated with a particular social position, and especially his interpretation of important contingencies as they were or will be encountered (Stebbins, 1970:34).

Although other influences present may modify this tendency, some people appear conceited about certain attainments in the early stages of their careers and proud of or modest about them during the later stages. In contrast to the veterans in the field, the accomplishments of a beginner are typically meager: he knows less, he has had fewer distinctive experiences, he has fewer achievements, and he has little reputation. In short, self-esteem here is built on a shaky foundation. It is also difficult to establish a sense of self-assurance on such a slight base. No wonder an individual at this stage in a career frets about the standing of his work in the eyes of certain audiences and thus manifests conceit. Indeed, this insecurity is probably strongest with regard to our most cherished roles, one of which is frequently occupation. For it is here that we invest the most time and energy and here that we expect to reap the greatest rewards. If they are not forthcoming, there is usually nowhere else to turn that has the same potential for self-satisfaction. In those situations where a doyen's behavior is defined by the audience as conceited, it is probable that similar psychological conditions prevail. Under these circumstances, the person is worried about the impression his work is making upon a specialized circle of outstanding members in the field or its sophisticated critics.

Still, it is obvious that most neophytes in a line of activity avoid conceited expression most of the time despite their lowly status in comparison with that of the veterans. This is possible because progress in a career, whatever the field of endeavor, is typically graded. One can achieve a measure of self-worth by excelling with reference to consensually recognized "bench marks" of advancement, even when they are early ones (Roth, 1963:12). Hence, even though graduation from music school can be considered only a good start for a professional musician, to have done so with honors is a source of satisfaction. This graduate knows he is far from the accomplishments of respected virtuosi, but his self-assurance is enhanced by the knowledge that his beginning is an auspicious one.

At this point, let us shift our attention to the positions of those in the audience. To the extent people choose to act proudly before one audience, modestly before another, and possibly even conceitedly (where intentional) before a third, they show a special alertness to the positions of those who comprise these audiences. Most of us are concerned that our achievements first be recognized and then be recognized as commendable. But this requires prudent selection of the audience before whom we decide to act proudly or conceitedly, for not everybody is impressed with a given accomplishment. Sometimes that accomplishment, though significant and praiseworthy to the actor, is perceived as unexceptional by a figure with long experience in the field who has forgotten what initial successes are like. Even those who would intentionally enact conceit must be circumspect about how they treat their audience. It is one thing, for example, to behave toward one's peers in this way - say, as a gesture of disdain - and quite another to do so before those who are admittedly superior. Conceit may be avoided in the latter situation, perhaps because the actor wishes to ingratiate himself (see Jones, 1964:ch. 1). If this is his aim, he must present an acceptable character; obnoxious conceit is hardly a sensible tactic.[14] For those who practice modesty under all or most circumstances, the question of structural composition of the audience should be largely irrelevant in this regard.

Put differently, the progress members of the audience are making or have made in their careers in the same field is a determinant of the choice to engage in modest, proud, or conceited talk. Military recruits strut with pride after successfuly proving themselves at certain tests of endurance and fortitude, but only, as a rule, before other recruits whose careers in the service are shorter.

Audiences comprised of such nonparticipants in the field as aficionados or recognized critics, or amateur participants or dilettanti also may encourage vainglorious speech from a person. Choice of the mode of expression, where aficionados or critics are concerned, seems to be influenced by the degree of specialized knowledge they are felt to possess for making judgments of excellence in that line of endeavor. A dilettante's actual accomplishments are likely to be an important consideration in addition to his expert knowledge. Where the level of knowledge or accomplishment is recognized by the actor as appreciably greater than his own, he will tend to avoid conceit for reasons already stated.

It is possible that we boast less of our achievements before those with whom we are on intimate terms (for example, close friends, relatives, marital partners) than before those whom we have just met, for intimates are already aware of our standing in various lines of activity. We may fish for compliments and compare outselves favorably with others when with intimates, but this is largely a search for role support from people who always have given it freely; such behavior is not conceit but a quest for reaffirmation.[15] On the other hand, first encounters are fertile ground for conceited and prideful behavior to take root in; where much of the conversation, if circumstances allow, centers in initial identification of others, which includes establishing their important attainments. The implication is that conceit especially, is an attempt to establish an initial and favorable evaluation of one's efforts, which is probably manifested in as many settings involving the same audience as the actor feels is necessary to achieve the desired image.

So far in this section, we have discussed only the actor's definition of the situation in which he expresses his self-esteem, approaching it from the structural standpoints of his career and his perception of the social positions of members of the audience. But there is also another side to the coin: the audience's view of the behavior of the actor. Specifically, whether his expressions of self-esteem are defined by members of the audience as modesty, pride, or conceit depends upon their own perception of their social positions as well. Readiness to describe another's behavior as fitting one of these three modes is partially contingent upon the stage they have reached in their own career in that line of activity. For instance, if they are beginners who lack experience and achievements, they, too, may be prone to notice the accomplishments of others and how they are generally rated and assessed. Consequently, someone speaking vainly about the exceptional quality and rank of his own work might be labeled quickly as conceited by such an audience, if for no other reason than to cut his self-regard down to proper size. By contrast, a person well along in his career and comfortable in his success, might regard the same behavior as a healthy expression of pride.

But the contrary is also possible: where the actor has high status within a field of activity and his audience low status (for example, celebrated professor in interaction with graduate students in his discipline), boasting by the actor may be reverently seen as a justified expression of pride by the audience. An audience of peers, on the other hand, might find the same utterances repugnant.

The speculations of the preceding two paragraphs are supported by data from a laboratory study by Jones and Shrauger (1970). They found that, for female undergraduates, a high self-evaluator tended to be more attractive than a low self-evaluator in the high reputation condition and a low self-evaluator tended to be more attractive than a high self-evaluator in the low reputation condition. Their definition of high self-evaluation is similar to the definition of pride used here; low self-evaluation is similar to our definition of self-debasing humility.

Situational Conditions

Expressions of modesty, pride, and conceit are influenced not only by the structural conditions or the status characteristics of those in the audience, but also by the nature of the occsion itself. Usually these three modes of expression appear as part of a larger encounter initiated for reasons independent of the maintenance and expression of self-esteem. Probably no type of interactive situation completely excludes the chance of some sort of discourse about personal attainment and hence the possibility of modest, proud, or conceited behavior. Nonetheless, some settings are more conducive to this sort of talk than are others. Successful expression of self-esteem, including modesty, appears to require time. We need conversational space in which to describe our achievements (or those of others), their strengths and weaknesses, their significance as determined by certain standards and specific achievements of others, and so forth. Therefore, it is suggested that emergency situations, hurried exchanges of all types, and strictly secondary relations typically fail to lend themselvs well to extended talk about personal effort.

Talk about high self-worth probably reaches its maximum expression in the ideal-type conversation refered to by Simmel (1949) as "sociability." In its pure form, sociability is the play form of association enjoyed for its intrinsic value. Sociable conversation guarantees the participants maximization of such values as joy, relief, and vivacity; it is democratic activity in the sense that the pleasure of one person is dependent upon that of others. Because it is a noninstrumental exchange between persons, sociability is destroyed by introducing wholly personal interests and goals and maintained by exhibiting amiability, proper breeding, cordiality, and attractiveness. In sociable conversation, one has time to deal with matters concerning self-esteem. It is hypothesized here, however, that conceited talk destroys its pleasurable aspects because such talk is founded entirely on personal interests and is scorned therefore by members of the audience. That it destroys sociable conversation only provides them with an additional reason for disliking it, especially when an expression of conceit or pride from one person stimulates reciprocal expression from one or more others present, leading to a contest of egotistic exchange.[16] In this connection, Gergen and Taylor (1969) found that laboratory subjects were likely to stress their positive qualities while in an occupational setting demanding productivity and likely to admit their shortcomings in an occupational setting demanding social compatibility.

Career-related events involving the actor and the members of the audience are also important situational conditions. The contingencies or special turning points in a person's career, by definition, contain special meaning. If they are favorable, such as in the example given earlier of the musician graduating from music school with honors, the individual may be tempted while the event is salient to thrust his self-satisfaction upon the audience. The audience, realizing the special significance of the event, also may relax its standards of propriety relating to expression of personal achievement and tolerate what would otherwise be disdained as vanity. Similarly, a member of the audience who has just experienced a favorable contingency might, as a result of his euphoria, be led to accept even conceited behavior from the actor, his frame of mind at the moment being such that he is unaffected by talk of this sort.

Further, whether an expression of self-esteem is defined as modesty, pride, or conceit depends upon how well it fits the overall conversation as it has progressed to that point in the encounter. For example, an achievement-centered remark that illustrates a general theme in the discussion is probably much less likely to be seen as conceit, or even pride, than one that enforces an abrupt change in the focus of talk. The latter is apt to be resented and quickly branded as vanity.

In this connection, it seems to make no difference who introduces the subject of the actor's personal achievement. The distinctive characteristics of modesty, pride, and conceit are found in the manner in which he responds to an introduction made by some member of the audience or in the manner in which he himself introduces the subject. It is possible to identify several types along both dimensions.

Let us turn first to the introduction of the topic of the actor's achievement by a member of the audience. Although possible only where the topic is introduced in a general way with no specific reference to the actor, he may choose to behave with modest secrecy or avoidance of public disclosure that he has achieved in this way. The golfer who has scored a hole in one sometime during his career but remains silent about it throughout discussion of the subject in the clubhouse illustrates this type.

When direct reference is made to his achievement, the actor may respond in one of at least three ways. He may invoke *modest rejection*: he takes no overt credit for the achievement. Instead, he passes the credit to someone else (for example, "Really, George did all the work") or pleasantly denies that the effort had any special merit (for example, "Oh, there was really nothing to it"). If, for reasons already mentioned, the actor wishes to express pride in his accomplishment, he acts with *proud acceptance* by taking public credit for his work in a socially acceptable manner. We often do this by thanking the complimenter politely and talking briefly about the strengths of the work and the events that led to its successful completion.[17] Finally, the actor may feel it is so important for him to impress the audience with the value of his accomplishment that he enacts *conceited acceptance* when the subject of it emerges in conversation. In so doing, he may embark upon an elaborate sequence of back-patting remarks (from the audience's point of view) and other forms of vanity designed to enhance his image, but usually leaving the others present with a feeling of regret for having mentioned the subject.

Turning to the type of situation where the actor himself introduces the topic of his accomplishment, we can start by noting that modest secrecy also may be selected here. He simply refrains from mentioning his exceptional efforts. Actual introduction of the topic may take several forms. In *modest display*, the accomplishment is introduced possibly because the actor is asked by a member of the audience if he has had certain experiences or reached certain levels of attainment, thereby permitting or forcing him to discuss his efforts briefly. For instance, a female college senior discussing training for professional acting might be asked how far she has progressed in her own schooling in this field, to which she could now reply that she is far beyond the critical first year - the year of "reality shock" (see Manning and Hearn, 1969). The actor subtly enters the subject of his accompishment into the conversation in *proud display*, with the hope that he will have an opportunity to discuss it in connection with his own work. At times it may even be possible to introduce the actual achievement without appearing conceited, as with our music student who had just graduated with honors. In *conceited display*, the actor injects into the conversation talk of his accomplishment and perhaps even the entire subject of it. This tactic is abrupt and therefore unwelcome; it upsets to a greater or lesser degree the smooth flow of discourse between participants.

Summary

I have attempted to provide a more comprehensive view of self-esteem by presenting some hypotheses about modesty, pride, and conceit as distinct modes of verbal behavior issuing from it. The nature of these three modes was discussed by differentiating each according to the amount and kind of discourse about the strengths and weaknesses of one's own achievements and the amount and kind of discourse about the strengths and weaknesses of related achievements of others. Conceit is conceptualized as a minor type of deviance, whereas pride and modesty are treated as more or less acceptable forms of expression of self-esteem.

Discussion of the structural and situational conditions for their expression followed, these conditions constituting a set of qualifications and further refinements to the basic statement of their nature. For various reasons, expressions of pride, and especially conceit, are influenced by the actor's position within the line of activity under consideration and his perception of the positions of those in the audience. Although many of the structural considerations for both the actor and the audience can be treated within the framework of subjective career, when dealing with the audience, other positions are important as well. Specifically, the expression of pride and conceit also depends upon whether or not those present are sophisticated or unsophisticated aficionados, critics, or dilettanti and whether or not they are intimates or fresh acquaintances.

Turning to the situational conditions for the expression of modesty, pride, and conceit, it was noted that, although these modes potentially can occur anywhere, they are most likely to be found in those settings in which there is adequate conversational time. The situation of sociable conversation is almost ideal in this respect. Certain other situational factors, such as currently salient career contingencies, nature of the conversation at that moment, and response to the manner of introduction of a topic of personal achievement were related to the expression and interpretation of modesty, pride, and conceit.

Endnotes

I.   By incorporating some of the research carried out by Edward Jones and Kenneth Gergen, this paper demonstrates how the concepts of modesty, pride, and conceit can help integrate hitherto theoretically unrelated studies of the expression of self-esteem.

2.   I wish to thank Ronald Joudrey for first suggesting this point to me. However, some physical movements, such as facial expressions and gestures, are coincident with speech about self-esteem. The nature and significance of the role they play as signs of the mode of expression being enacted must be determined by empirical investigation.

3.   When speaking of the accomplishments of others as an aspect of modesty, pride, and conceit, it is imperative to maintain the actor's achievements as the focus. Otherwise, we are easily led away from these three modes of expression into criticism and evaluation as they relate to other orientations, such as backbiting, gossip, impersonal professional criticism, and the like.

4.   This definition of audience is identical to that presented by Goffman (1961: 85-152) in his essay on role distance.

5.   For the sake of simplicity, I am considering situations in which there is only one audience. Most readers, however, can undoubtedly think of occasions when they have been confronted by multiple audiences requiring more than one of these modes of expression of self-esteem.

6.   Humility, when it connotes self-respect, can be taken as more or less synonymous with modesty.

7.   This follows from the definition of audience given above. As pointed out in the remaining two sections of this paper, there are probably times when the actor feels his behavior, though conceited in other contexts, is excused for various reasons in the present one. And there are other times, perhaps, when the actor cares little, or not at all, about the audience's opinion of his behavior, in which case conceit can be enacted with impunity. The practice of "putting on" another person could involve behavior of this sort, where both actor and audience share the definition of the actor's behavior as conceited. But intentional conceit is rare in real life, which is probably why it is so frequently and effectively used in fiction and

theater. The vanity of Pooh Bah in Sir William Gilbert's The Mikado, for instance, would be intolerable in actuality and hence unlikely to be expressed.

8.   The principles of decorum appear to root in our Judeo-Christian heritage and more recently in the spirit of modern democracy. More precisely, they seem to be, in part, a more pointed expression of the social values of considerateness of others, leniency in dealing with their mistakes, and fairness in our treatment of them. Pine-Coffin arrives at a similar conclusion in his introduction to Della Casa (1958: 10).

9.   Concerning the nearly ideal conformity of modesty, it is noteworthy that this word stems from the Latin term modestus, which means keeping oneself within measure or keeping well regulated.

10.   Although there may be a certain amount of validity to this impression—the actor is generally believed to have performed exceptionally in some degree—we still may scorn vainglorious reference to this fact by such people. But, as pointed out in the next paragraph, the actor is seen as failing to see this collective opinion; he is uncertain of the audience's evaluation of his accomplishments.

11.   Argyle (1967:127) has made the same observation in a discussion about seeking self-esteem.

12.   Several observations in this paper are similar, in some respects, to those of Cooley. His discussion, however, suffers from the tendency to consider pride and vanity as aspects of character, rather than as situated behavioral expressions pertaining to specified accomplishments.

13.   Although there is insufficient space to report it here, the author did carry out a small research project designed to illustrate the principal observations just made on the nature of modesty, pride, and conceit. There is, to the author's knowledge, no research or secondary resource material that treats modesty, pride, and conceit in such a way as to constitute an adequate illustration of their main characteristics. Without an illustration, however, there is the chance their meaning and relationships will remain unclear for some. Consequently, three fictitious incidents were developed by the author for judgment by a group of subjects. Each incident exemplifies the observations just made on the nature of modesty, pride, and conceit. From their experience, 73 subjects (university students in an

introductory sociology course) were able to identify as modesty, pride, or conceit the fictitious incidents of these modes when presented to them on stenciled forms. Besides supporting the conceptions of modesty, pride, and conceit presented here, these data also demonstrate and support the relationship of these three modes to each other. A report of this research and a copy of the stenciled forms distributed to the subjects are available from the author upon request.

14. Preference for a certain composition of audience implies, though the actor may be chagrined to discover this, that its opinion of his efforts is important enough to him to warrant interacting with and trying to impress. In this respect, conceit may be compared with snobbery, which is either a refusal to interact with the audience or, if association with them is unavoidable, a form of superficial interaction designed to maintain maximum social distance. Of course, this interpretation depends upon the insight of the audience. Its members may fail to perceive such behavior in this light, owing to the distracting repugnance of conceit.

15. The difference between a quest for reaffirmation and an instance of conceit is subtle, but important. Because the person who is expected to give the role support is known to the actor for having done so freely in the past, little more than a hint is believed to be needed in order to gain this sort of reward again. Glaring conceit is hardly necessary. With acquaintances and people one has just met, some actors feel a hint is not enough; these people must be informed directly of given attainments and their merits.

16. A reciprocal exchange of expressions of modesty should militate against such an occurrence. These observations are supported by experimental data (see Gergen and Wishnov, 1965).

17. In this situation, proud behavior may be nearly as acceptable as modesty, because the actor corroborates the judgment of the complimenter by explaining why his achievement should be commended. In this way, the complimenter's sense of self-worth is enhanced as well.

References

Argyle, Michael
  1967   The Psychology of Interpersonal Behaviour. Harmondsworth, Eng.: Penguin.

Della Casa, Giovanni
  1958   Galateo: or the Book of Manners. (R. S. Pine-Coffin, trans.) Harmondsworth, Eng.:Penguin.

Cooley, Charles H.
  1922   Human Nature and the Social Order. New York: Schocken.

Gergen, Kenneth J. and Margaret G. Taylor
  1969   "Social expectancy and self- presentation in a status hierarchy." J. of Experimental Social Psychology 5 (January):79-92.

Gergen, Kenneth J. and Barbara Wishnov
  1965   "Others' self-evaluations and interaction anticipation as determinants of self-presentation." J. of Personality and Social Psychology 2 (September):348-358.

Goffman, Erving
  1956   "The nature of defence and demeanor." Amer. Anthropologist 58 (June):473-502.
  1961   Encounters. Indianpolis:Bobbs- Merril.

Hockart, A.M.
  1931   "Etiquette." Pp. 615-617 in Volume 5 of Edwin R.A. Seligman and Alvin Johnson (eds.) Encyclopedia of the Social Sciences. New York: Macmillan.

Jones, Edward E.
  1964   Ingratiation. New York: Appleton-Century-Crofts.

Jones, Stephen C. and J. Sidney Shrauger
  1970   "Reputation and self-evaluation as determinants of attractiveness." Sociometry 33 (September):276-286.

Manning, Peter K. and H.L. Hearn
  1969   "Student actresses and their artistry." Social Forces 48 (December):202-213.

Maurois, Andre
1930 Conversation. (Yvonne Dufour, trans.) New York: E.P. Dutton.

Mead, George H.
1934 Mind, Self, and Society. Chicago: Univ. of Chicago Press.
1938 The Philosophy of the Act. Chicago: Univ. of Chicago Press.

Pear, T. H.
1939 The Psychology of Conversation. London: Thomas Nelson.

Post, Emily
1957 Etiquette: The Blue Book for Social Usage. New York: Funk & Wagnalls.

Roth, Julius A.
1963 Timetables, Indianapolis: Bobbs- Merril.

Simmel Georg
1949 "The sociology of sociability." Amer. J. of Sociology 55 (November):254-261.

Stebbins, Robert A.
1970 "Career: the subjective approach." Soc. Q. 11 (Winter):32-49.

Chapter 7

ROLE DISTANCE

In contrast to the majority of the participants, my observations reveal that
Bea, a talkative, middle-class woman of 78, was one of the five individuals who displayed role distancing behavior. She first came to the group
[class] as a participant and did not like . . . [it]. She returned, three weeks
later calling herself a volunteer. Bea told the researcher that she did not
consider herself part of the group because she felt intellectually superior.
Unlike them, she could never "sit and do nothing all day." Most of her
conversations stressed how busy she was and described the different
activities in which she had been engaged throughout her life. It was
important to Bea that staff and other clients see her as busy and not as an
inactive client (Marnie L. Sayles. Role Distancing: Differentiating the
Role of the Elderly from the Person. *Qualitative Sociology* 7 (1984):236-
52).

It has been seven years since Erving Goffman published his essay on
role distance in *Encounters*.[1] Perhaps one of his most original and
insightful contributions to sociology and social psychology, there has been
during this period a surprisingly small amount of empirical research on this
subject, although some sporadic discussion of it has occurred.[2] There are
at least two reasons for this lack of interest: (1) Goffman's own formulation is logically vague and ambiguous and (2) the nature of role distance
makes investigation of it difficult. Our objectives here are to resolve as
much of this vagueness and ambiguity as is possible and desirable at this
stage of theoretical development and to suggest ways in which research
might be carried out on this phenomenon. Observations on role distance

*The author wishes to express his gratitude to Professor John W. Prehn whose
coments and suggestions have added much of value to his paper.

and role distance behaviour among jazz musicians will be used to illustrate our points.

The very definition of role distance which is presented by Goffman in the course of ten pages, often by means of the liberal use of example, is the principal source of confusion.[3] Yet, upon careful perusal of this section of his essay it beomes clear that the defining elements of this idea are present, needing only to be collected into a more coherent statement. Role distance develops in connection with a particular status or identity and, more specifically, in connection with all or part of its associated role expectations. Role distance which is part of the individual's interpretation of these expectations reflects a desire to dissociate himself from them, the reason for this being traceable to their threat to his self-conception.[4] The inclination to engage in role distance behaviour is stimulated by the presence of a certain 'audience' or special other persons in the ongoing situation who will denigrate the role player for enacting the expectations. However, such behaviour should not be conceived as a refusal to play out those expectations. Rather it is best seen as an adaptive strategy, whereby the performer can more or less fulfil his role obligations while maintaining his self-respect.

The idea of role distance is not so abstract and complex as to preclude a more formal definition of it. Indeed such is required in order to bring together the essential elements which make up this concept and to minimize ambiguity and confusion. Thus, role distance can be defined as an attitude of dislike toward all or part of a set of role expectations which, when enacted, bring the threat of a loss of respect and at least momentary lack of support for one's self-conception from certain reference others present in the situation.[5] The role distance attitude is to be distinguished from the actual performance expressing this predisposition which we shall call *role-distance behaviour* or *taking role distance*.

That Goffman's presentation of the defining qualities of role distance has spawned confusion is evident in the few papers which have followed his. Levitin never does grasp the fact that role distance is expressed in behaviour before an audience of reference others and not, as he thinks, before sub-categories of customers whom the puller[6] is trying to convince to enter the store to make a purchase. It is doubtful that any of his examples are instances of taking role distance since the customers are clearly not reference others to the puller, and he certainly does not need to convince himself that specific expectations in his occupational role threaten his self-esteem. If there is an audience of reference others, it is either the salesmen within the store or other pullers down the street. But they are not mentioned in this capacity.[7]

Elsewhere, the author has discussed in greater detail the significance of the threat of enacting certain expectations to the actor's self-conception. This theme is present, though rather dimly, in Goffman's essay. Its relative obscurity there seems to have led Rose Coser to overlook this important aspect of role distance in her attempt to relate it to sociological ambivalence and transitional status systems.[8]

The shortcomings in the treatment of role distance by Ford, Young, and Box can also be attributed to the inadequacies of Goffman's initial statement. However, before we consider their ideas it will facilitate our aims if we draw some new distinctions. First of all, we can differentiate 'major role distance' from 'minor role distance'. The former refers to the attitude which develops toward highly threatening expectations. They are usually perceived in this way because they are associated with an identity *high* in the person's salience hierarchy. The latter refers to the attitude toward moderate or only slightly threatening expectations. These expectations relate to an identity *low* in the salience hierarchy; or regardless of the position of the identity, their enactment makes a person appear oddly different from the reference others in some more or less trivial way. One might appear trivially different from others by being identified as liking expectations generally defined as boring, difficult, or physically uncomfortable. The salience hierarchy is the situational rearrangement of the actor's overall prominence or importance hierarchy of his total set of identities or statuses.[9]

A distinction between kinds of role-distance behaviour will also prove beneficial. We shall use the term 'true role-distance behaviour' to refer to actions which are an expression of a genuine role-distance attitude (major or minor). The expectations are genuinely disliked, and the actor does not wish the reference others present to get the impression that he likes them. 'False role-distance behaviour' shall designate actions which are *not* an expression of a genuine role-distance attitude. Instead the actor tries to create the impression that he holds this attitude while, in fact, he is actually attracted to the expectations.

Getting back to the paper by Ford and her associates, we are told that role distance is not possible to any significant degree among lower-class people because they lack the skills necessary to step outside their roles, beause they 'receive' rather than 'interpret' their norms (they are bound by 'rulefulness'), and because they have 'total' friendships with each other.[10] These assertions can be challenged on the following grounds, most of which are misunderstandings of the nature of role distance. Thus, if taking role distance is impossible because of total interpersonal relationships, then this can only pertain to false role-distance behaviour rather than to the true variety. The high level of intimate knowledge characteristic of such relationships is a barrier only to dissimulative behaviour. True role-distance behaviour expresses a genuinely held attitude.

Moreover, though not mentioned explicitly by Goffman, it seems to this author that there is usually the requirement - very much a part of the set of role expectations of an identity - that one will hold a role-distance attitude toward certain other expectations and behave accordingly. If those in the lower-classes are bound by rulefulness, they must also be bound by this rule. By way of caveat it should be noted that it is not true as Coser believes that role distance is itself part of the normative framework; it is part of the interpretation of that framework, although an interpretation which is expected by the reference others.[11] This feature will be evident in our observations on jazz musicians to be presented shortly. Finally, if lower-class people are expected to hold role-distance attitudes towards certain role requirements, then it is not unreasonable to assume that in the course of their socialization, they will also learn the techniques for expressing these dispositions just as they learned the expectation that they should have them in the first place.

So far we have been engaged in identifying and attempting to resolve some of the confusion created by Goffman's presentation of the fundamentals of role distance. One other factor was also cited as inhibiting research on this subject: namely, the difficulties involved in studying empirically such a subjective phenomena. It is obvious that the modes of expression of role distance will vary widely from community to community and from subculture to subculture within any one community. Consequently, the researcher is forced to gain an intimate knowledge of the group under study before he can make any meaningful statements about when role distance occurs and how it is externalized for the benefit of reference others. An extensive amount of participant observation is clearly a prerequisite for empirical investigation of role distance anywhere except in circles well known to the social scientist. Furthermore, since instances of role-distance behaviour are probably only a small proportion of the total number of acts performed by an individual, observational research conducted expressly for the purpose of studying role distance may be relatively unrewarding because the return is so low. Indeed, it is probably better to include this interest in a larger investigation, such as some sort of participant observer form of community study.

The observations on jazz musicians reported below do not wholly comply with these suggestions. They are based upon the author's participation in jazz music over a period of ten years in two communities in which a close acquaintance was developed with the associated sub-culture.[12] But, gathering data on role distance and role distance behaviour was never part of a larger study design, so that the observations recorded here are somewhat less systematic than is desirable. Still, the historical nature of jazz musical life in the two cities lends a good measure of confidence to the generality of the observations even though we may be unable to give much precision to the frequency of the occurrence of role-distance behavour.[13]

Role Distance Among Jazz Musicians

At least six general modes or role-distance behaviour can be identified:

1. Presence of special vocal behaviour: e.g., grunts, speech, laughs, etc.
2. Absence of ordinary vocal behaviour
3. Presence of special gestures: e.g., face, hands, body movements, etc.
4. Absence of ordinary gestures
5. Presence of special deeds
6. Absence of ordinary deeds

By the phrase 'presence of special vocal behaviour' (gestures or deeds) is meant simply that these expressions are manifestations of a role-distance attitude toward certain expectations salient at the moment. Because it is 'special' behaviour should not lead one to lose sight of the fact that some meaningful mode of taking role distance is expected by the reference others. Also, the phrase 'absence of ordinary vocal behaviour' (gestures or deeds) merely refers to the withholding of certain usual practices as an expression of role distance. Again such withholding behaviour is expected by the reference others. Lastly, it should be apparent that modes 1 and 2, 3 and 4, 5 and 6 are not in any way dichotomous. The use of these modes by jazz musicians is evident in the following description of two major role-distance attitudes which are expected of them at certain times during musical performances.

One of these attitudes lies behind the jazz musician's reaction to the expectation that he play the 'tunes' or songs requested by the listening audience. This is not an objectionable requirement as long as the requests are recognized as appropriate jazz fare. But in an unknown but distressingly large proportion of such instances this is not the case. Non-jazz numbers are requested which are referred to as 'square tunes' or some uncomplimentary equivalent (e.g., old-time waltzes and polkas, folk songs, many popular songs, rock and roll hits, etc.), and are regarded with great scorn by the true artist. Under these circumstances the individual jazz musician is expected by other jazz musicians present, whether they are in the band or in the audience, to exhibit role-distance behaviour.

The vocal behaviour mode of expression is widely used. The choice of words and the tone of voice used in communication among those in the band convey their disgust as they pass the news of the loathed request to each other, commenting upon it as they do so. Even the speech and tone of voice of the band leader in conversation with the requester may be freighted with externalizations of role distance directed less at the requester himself than at reference others present. Equally prominent and usually accompanying vocal behaviour are certain hand and facial gestures, such as a thumbs down motion, a frown, an expression denoting an odious gustatory taste, and the like. During the actual playing of the maligned tune, members of the band may take further role distance by displaying complete disinterest (e.g., placid face, eyes shut as if asleep), or, if possible, engage in other activities with their spare hands, such as drinking beer, smoking a cigarette, toying with one's clothing, or even scratching parts of the body. These obvious signs of disinterest are simultaneously an example of the absence of gestures, sine the performance of a jazz tune there is considerable evidence of concentration and outright enjoyment, if not ecstasy.

On occasion certain deeds may be employed to express this role-distance attitude. Hence, one or more of the musicians may intentionally 'jazz up' the square tune even though this makes for poor jazz itself. That jazz musicians and knowledgeable buffs present recognize the significance of this action is evident by the round of laughter and chuckles from those in the room who are 'hip' or aware of the intended meaning. The very stalling of the playing of the requested square tune can be seen as the absence of an expected deed full of in-group significance. The musicians may also demonstrate their disinterest during the performance by talking to one another, not infrequently telling jokes or some colourful anecdote about mutual musical acquaintances.

Somewhat less regular in occurrence but often even more disliked, is the request by some member of the audience to 'sit-in' for two or three numbers and sing with the band. If, in fact, the singer is good this is heartily welcomed, but usually the capable singers in a community are known and if present they will be invited to sing. When the singer is reputed to be poor or the state of his talent is unknown, jazz musicians fear the worst and react accordingly. These reactions include most if not all of the expressions employed in playing square tunes.[14] In addition, there will usually be a noticeable absence of such vocal behaviour as compliments (unless the singer is young and is perceived as working to improve) and any mention of further opportunities to sing with the band. If the person who asks to sit-in is a musician instead of a singer but is still defined as square, a member of the band may express role distance by suggesting a square tune to play while he is performing with them. This is doubly significant since jazz musicians who sit-in are conventionally allowed to select the tune themselves because they are in the role of honoured guest instead of intruder. An amusing but more idiosyncratic practice of expressing role distance when such intruders appear was used by a piano player known to the author who delighted in signalling the exit of such people from the bandstand by playing the song 'Fine and Dandy' at a fast tempo - a rendition of a tune traditionally employed by musicians providing the exit music for stripteasers at the end of their performance.

Although there may be others these are the two most prevalent major role-distance attitudes of the jazz musician in his capacity as musical performer. The repugnancies of square music and square musicians are both social-psychological manifestations of the omnipresent problem of the tension between art and commercialism which characterizes the jazz life.[15]

Minor Role Distance & Role-Distance Behavior

Several minor role-distance attitudes develop out of the occupational life of jazz musicians. Many of these are connected with the working conditions of the jazz job where, for instance, one is expected to be ready to play at a certain time in the evening (punctuality) and to be in such physical condition as to finish in good form four to six hours later. This often includes employment under considerably less than ideal circumstances, like being expected to perform on undersized bandstands, on dilapidated and out-of-tune pianos, in excessive heat and cigarette smoke, with faulty electronic equipment, and so forth.[16] Jazz musicians generally do not care for many or all of these requirements of their work. But, even if one should take pride in his punctuality or show such unusual exuberance for the music that he is not even ready to quit six hours later, his reference others do not take this as evidence of a major blemish in his character. He is simply regarded as a bit different ('somewhat of a nut') in a world characterized by extensive tolerance for unusual personalities.[17]

Additionally, jazz musicians typically show a dislike for individual practice on their musical instruments, an attitude which probably exists in many other categories of musicians as well. When talk about practising comes up, one is expected to take role distance, and it is this authors observation that many do.

The fact that some of the serious, hard-working jazz musicians do not object to but often enjoy their individual practice sessions leads to instances of false role-distance behaviour. They do not usually do a very good job of dissembling, however, for their occasional weak expressions of supposed role distance are more than overbalanced by their insistence in conversation that practice is the key to success and by their rather steady improvement. There is in fact a certain amount of ambivalence about individual practice in jazz communities; the one who does this extensively is regarded as different in a strange but admirable way. The respected musician is a competent musician, and he arrives at this position through no other route than by constant hard work on his instrument. It is also this person who commands the greatest influence in local jazz circles.[18]

Another occasion for false role-distance behaviour is found in the situation where the jazz musician is involved in playing 'legit' music or that which he must read instead of improvise. Because a large proportion of jazz musicians are poor readers[19] they often scorn music made in this manner and consequently scorn those who enjoy playing it. Yet, a smaller percentage of jazz musicians are able readers and they find pleasure in successfully playing music which is difficult from this point of view. Nonetheless, they often discover that they must feign role-distance behaviour here in order to avoid a certain amount of loss of respect. It is true that some types of reading are more undesirable than others because the expectation that the jazz musician will play only improvised music is roughly related to the degree of commercialism involved. It is wonderful if the musician can read the musical scores written for big jazz bands or even for small combos (both of which involve some improvisation as well). It is less so if he shows an interest in the classical side of music, and it is heresy if he likes reading polka music (which is very challenging) or something else designed for mass consumption.

In these cases of minor role distance and false role-distance behaviour, the variety in the modes of expression is considerably less than in major role distane. Theoretically, this is to be expected from the fact that there is much less of a threat here for the individual's self-conception. From our jazz observations, attitudes of minor role distance appear to be weak, partly because they are not congruent with other attitudes of similar strength. Therefore, ambivalence may be characteristic of a person's orientation toward certain role expectations leading him to take role distance at some points and to avoid such behaviour at others. One does not greatly elaborate the externalizations of his role distance under such conditions since he is not sure of his own sentiments toward the expectations.

Summary and Conclusions

In response to the observation that the current state of theoretical and descriptive development of the concept of role distance has led to a paucity of research and to an abundance of confusion, the following aims were pursued: to try to resolve some of the vagueness and ambiguity inherent in Goffman's initial definition and explanation and to suggest a few ways in which research can be carried out on this phenomenon. A concise definition of role distance was presented and differentiated from role-distance behaviour. Additional distinctions were made between kinds of role distance (major and minor) and between types of role-distance behaviour (false and true). Research in this area is hampered by the time consuming necessity of gaining an intimate knowledge of the culture or subculture where role distance is to be studied and by the fact that the occurrence of role distance is probably relatively infrequent. It was suggested that the best strategy to meet these obstacles was to incorporate this research interest as part of a larger participant observer study. By way of illustration some observations on role distance among jazz musicians were presented within the framework of six modes of role-distance behaviour. They were found to hold both major and minor role-distance attitudes and to take true and false role distance on various occasions.

The importance of role distance and role-distance behaviour for the man of modern mass society is put most picturesquely by Peter Berger. Role distance, properly expressed, promotes 'ecstasy' or 'the act of standing or stepping outside [literally, *ekstasis*] the taken-for-granted routines of society', and ecstasy in turn leads to a transformation of our awareness of everyday life.[20] Not only do we gain a new perspective, but we have exercised our will in the process, thereby informing ourselves that we are not completely the automatons that so much of life seems to suggest.

Contrary to the views of Ford, Young, and Box the arguments advanced in this paper seem to retain something of the voluntarist flavour both for lower-class men and for symbolic interactionist theory.[21] True it is not a totally voluntaristic view; few responsible social scientists would take such a position today. But rather it is a 'soft determinism', to borrow David Matza's phrase, where man is neither completely free nor wholly determined.[22] Our ecstatic man taking role distance is exercising his limited choice by selecting between the perspectives offered him by his various reference groups and by expressing himself through those modes of role-distance behaviour which are personally most appropriate. When two reference-group perspectives clash, and that is often in modern life even among a substantial proportion of the lower classes, he has no alternative but to act in harmony with one or the other or to improvise some sort of intermediate stand. The reference others in the audience will have a significant effect upon his choice. But, in electing to take role distance in order to maintain their support of his self-image, he has simultaneously stepped out of part or all of the other role and rejected the perspective of its reference group.

Endnotes

1. Erving Coffman, Encounters, Indianapolis, Ind., The Bobbs-Merrill Co., 1961, pp. 85—152.

2. To this author's knowledge, there is only one empirical investigation of role distance: that of Levitin, a case study of a single clothing store 'puller' in Chicago. See T. E. Levitin, 'Role Performance and Role Distance in a Low Status Occupation: The Puller', Sociological Quarterly, vol. 5, no. 3 (1964), pp. 251–60. Discursive articles have been produced by Rose Coser, 'Role Distance, Sociological Ambivalence, and Transitional Status Systems', Amer. J. Sociol., vol. 72 (1966), pp. 173— 187; Robert A. Stebbins, 'A Note on the Concept of Role Distance', Amer. J. Sociol., vol. 73, no. 2 (1967), pp. 247-250; Julienne Ford, Douglas Young, and Steven Box, 'Functional Autonomy, Role Distance, and Social Class', Brit. J. Sociol., vol. 18, no. 4 (1967), pp. 370–81.

3. Goffman, op. cit., pp. 105-15.

4. As part of the interpretation of role expectations, role distance is an aspect of what Pugh calls the 'role conception'. See Derek Pugh, 'Role Activation Conflict: A Study of Industrial Inspection', Amer. Sociol. Rev., vol. 31, no. 6 (1966), p. 836.

5. Coser introduced the idea of reference group to the role-distance framework (op. cit., p. 174). Stebbins contributed the idea that role distance is really an attitude toward role expectations (op. cit., p. 250).

6. Levitin describes a puller as 'a salesman who stations himself outside the store for which he works, selects potential customers from passing individuals, and persuades them to enter the store, where other salesmen assist them in selecting merchandise' (op. cit., p. 251).

7. Ibid., passim. Supporting the contention that Goffman's formulation of role distance is vague and ambiguous, is the observation that a committee of sociologists selected this paper for First Prize in the Manford H. Kuhn Memorial Essay Contest for students held each year by the Midwest Sociological Society in the United States.

8. Stebbins, op. cit.; Coser, op. cit.

9. We rank our identities by their significance to us in general, but in specific ongoing settings we may modify this ranking to some extent as a result of the influences of others present. For a further discussion of these ideas, see George J. McCall and J. L. Simmons, Identities and Interactions, New York, The Free Press, 1966, pp. 76–87.

10. Ford, et al., op. cit.

11. Possibly it is true that individual members of lower-class groups receive far more than they interpret rules. What is being suggested here is that they also receive an interpretation of rules which may be quite different from that held by other segments of the community or by other reference groups of which they are members. This, of course, also pertains to the person who is socially mobile; he is receiving interpretations from the group he aspires to join.

12. Roughly four of the ten years were spent performing on a regular professional basis in the historically significant Minneapolis jazz community.

13. The observations made on role distance in Minneapolis are supported by subsequent observations made in St. John's, Newfoundland. Jazz and jazz musicians in this latter city have a very diversified background, developing largely around musicians in a United States Air Force Band stationed there during and after the Second World War. Since these musicians were recruited from all parts of the United States, role distance among today's jazz musicians in St. John's can be said to have a wide base.

14. When the singer is unknown jazz musicians may delay their role-distance behaviour until he shows his talent. A number of cues are used to predict how he will perform, and they influence whether or not a musician takes role distance immediately or waits with guarded suspicion.

15. For a discussion of art versus commercialism in jazz, see Howard S. Becker, 'The Professional Dance Musician and His Audience', Amer. J. Sociol., vol. 57 (1951), pp. 140–1; Robert A. Stebbins, 'The Conflict Between Musical and Commercial Values in the Minneapolis Jazz Community', Proc. Minnesota Acad. Sci., vol. 30, no. 1 (1962)-pp. 75–9; William Bruce Cameron, 'Sociological Notes on the Jam Session', Social Forces, vol. 33 (1954), p. 182.

16. These expectations are first of all those of nightclub management; but jazz musicians, knowing the state of the market, also expect their colleagues not to be overly fastidious in this respect.

17. Cameron, Merriam and Mack, and Stebbins all express this theme of the greater tolerance for unusual personalities and behaviour found within the jazz community as compared to the larger urban milieu. See Cameron, op. cit., p. 181; A. P. Merriam and R. W. Mack, 'The Jazz Community', Social Forces, vol. 38 (1960), p. 218; Robert A. Stebbins, 'Class, Status, and Power among Jazz and Commercial Musicians, Sociological Quarterly, vol. 7, no. 2 (1966), p. 206.

18. Stebbins, 'Class, Status, and Power among Jazz and Commercial Musicians', op. cit., pp. 208–9; Robert A. Stebbins, 'A Theory of the Jazz Community', Sociological Quarterly vol. 9, no. 3 (1968), p. 328.

19. Although this is less true today than at any time in the past, a majority are still to be considered bad readers.

20. Peter L. Berger, An Invitation to Sociology, Garden City, N.Y., Doubleday & Co., 1963, pp. 135–7.

21. Ford. et al., op. cit., pp. 377–8.

22. David Matza, Delinquency and Drift, New York, John Wiley & Sons, 1964, ch. 1. See also Arnold M. Rose's eight qualifications to cultural determinism in Human Behavior and Social Processes, Boston, Houghton Mifflin Co., 1962, pp. 14–15.

Chapter 8

HUMOUR

> The [class] clown offered more than just comic relief. He was threatening
> in the way he symbolically stripped the teachers naked and demythologized
> the classroom power structure. . . . Because he was often amusing, the
> clown was not perceived as a direct threat, yet his antics could not go
> totally unpunished. . . . The clown demanded that the teacher laugh at
> himself or herself and all that the teacher represented. To a certain extent
> teachers met this demand. . . for fear of incurring extended antics from the
> clown or reprisals from other, more dangerous students (Peter McLaren.
> *Schooling as a Ritual Performance*. London: Routledge & Kegan Paul, p.
> 160).

Our preoccupation with the serious side of schooling has led us away
from the role that humour plays in classroom life. That pupils are able to
tolerate and even enjoy primary and secondary education may be related
as much to the laughter they can find in the classroom as to the sense of their
own self-actualisation and self-expression. They certainly consider it
important for, in the later grades, they compare their teachers on this
dimension, just as they do on such dimensions as fairness, leniency, and
strictness.[1]

So far as humour is concerned, teachers themselves were once divided
over the question of whether or not to smile or permit their pupils to do so.[2]
Even among those who felt that humour has a place in the schoolroom,
some held that one should start off in a serious mood, just to establish
firmly who is boss, and only gradually drift toward a more jocular
disposition as the term wears on. Others operated by the rule of thumb that
one should 'never smile before Christmas'.

Even today, teachers are being exhorted by several writers to inject more humour into their classroom proceedings.[3] Still, there are gaps in our knowledge about the role of humour in this setting, gaps that must be filled if such advice is to be effectively heeded. It is pointed out later in this chapter that the functions of classroom humour have recently come under a certain amount of empirical scrutiny. But the social psychology of this behaviour has been less adequately explored. And nowhere is the sociology of classroom humour given systematic theoretical treatment.

By way of theoretical backdrop, the classroom may be viewed as an example of what Goffman calls a 'situated activity system'[4]. The central activity in these systems is said to occur entirely within the walls of a single social establishment where the individual (teacher) is brought face-to-face with others (pupils) for the performance of a single joint endeavour (teaching-learning). The events in a situated activity system are more or less closed to outsider participation and are limited in time. In it individual participants acquire situated selves based on roles they play and on the 'sign vehicles' that convey expressions and impressions of those selves.

As Goffman points out, the standard roles availabale to participants in these systems may constrain their expressions of self.[5] That is, certain misinformation or lack of information about their feelings, attitudes, opinions, beliefs, and the like gets uncontrollably communicated (or omitted) through the sign vehicles which, if the participants are aware of it, they wish to correct. Though Goffman is less clear on this point, it is conceivable that such corrections on the part of, say, teachers, can have functional consequences for the overall activity system.

It is my contention that humour is one important type of sign vehicle that teachers may use (though they may sometimes fail to recognise its use for this purpose) to correct or supplement information about themselves that was communicated in earlier behaviour. Because teachers are so significant a part of the classroom situated activity system, their humorous expressions of self may also be viewed as strategies that affect the tenor of events in the immediate present of that system.

Practically speaking, teachers who wish to use humour as a strategy to facilitate instruction or maintain order should have a rudimentary understanding of the sociological processes connected with it. For humour, when inappropriately used, may only worsen relations with pupils.

For teachers in the classroom then, humour has, at the very least, two roles: that of strategy and that of self-expression. For the most part it appears to serve in them simultaneously. This chapter opens with an examination of the strategic role of the functional consequences of teachers' humour in the immediate present. We then work backwards through the causal chain to the social psychological processes of classroom humour and its potential and actual use by teachers to inform pupils, intentionally or unintentionally, about their situated selves. Lastly, the concrete forms of classroom humour are described. These are the sign vehicles by which earlier inadequately communicated or uncommunicated information about self can be corrected or added.

Functions of Classroom Humour

Paralleling the call for more humour in the classroom is a growing research interest in identifying and describing the sociological or system maintaining functions of jokes and other forms of humour used among teachers and their pupils. Several participant observer studies focusing partly or wholly on humour have been conducted.[6] A perusal of these works indicates that they deal with one or more of the three broad functions of humour - conflict, control, and consensus - abstracted and elucidated by Martineau in his review of all sociological research on this subject.[7]

The strategic role of humour in these functions is obvious. Conflict humour is essentially an act of aggression through which a noxious stimulus is delivered at someone or some group.[8] As noted in the next section it differs from control humour in its antecedent definition of the humour situation. Control humour, such as that expressed in satire or ridicule, though noxious itself at times, springs from a different motive. It is designed to prevent behaviour that the humorous person disdains and that may drive him to engage in conflict humour should such behaviour actually occur. In consensual humour a solidarity or bonhomie is created; the social interaction exudes a warm feeling of good-natured friendliness. It is possible, of course, that a particular humorous event or act could function in more than one of these ways.

Elsewhere I have advanced a fourth function of humour, which I call 'social comic relief'.[9] Being the everyday analogue of the theatric kind, it is found in various settings including schoolrooms. Comic relief offers a mementary respite from the seriousness of lengthy concentration on a collective task, a respite that facilitates the completion of that task by refreshing the participants. Those involved also feel compelled to stay at the task. That is, they have no socially acceptable means of escape from the setting of concentration, such as by quitting before the task is finished, going into reverie, or even taking a short break. In the usual case the time within which to complete the task is limited. Put otherwise, social comic relief reduces fatigue which, if allowed to increase, threatens role performance and motivation.[10]

For comic relief to take place certain conditions pertaining to *concentration* must be met. Concentration is (1) required to reach a goal, (2) collective - involving two or more people, (3) lengthy, (4) forced - affording no socially acceptable form of escape, (5) limited to a period of time. Additionally, laughter must occur as indicative of a break in this concentration, a break that revitalises and thereby facilitates the group in completing its task.

In the classroom any form of humour, whether introduced by the teacher or a pupil, could potentially provide social comic relief, assuming the five conditions of concentration are met and the act is judged humorous. The presentation of a lesson is the main activity in which comic relief is likely to occur in the typical schoolroom. Before this point, examinations, individual study, and presentations engaged in or received may have contributed to student mental fatigue. Consequently, humour that functions as comic relief should be most frequent toward the end of the school day or toward the end of the week.[11]

Two examples taken from the participant observation literature on clssroom interaction must suffice to illustrate the comic relief function. The first centres on a practical joke initiated by a student:

> Three grade seven boys were sitting one in front of the other at the far end of a row of desks that adjoined a blackboard located on one side of the classroom. The discussion about whole numbers was growing more and more tiresome. So, when the teacher turned her back to write on another blackboard at the front of the room, Kevin who sat in the last desk slouched in his seat, sighted along the chalky tray, and blew gently. The small cloud of chalk dust that arose drifted silently down the tray past Carl in the next desk to Max two desks away. At this point the cloud suddenly turned, as if guided by an invisible hand, and encircled Max's head. The reaction was predictable. Max, a somewhat gangling boy with a long, narrow face and large ears, promptly sensed what was expected by his peers; he began to cough and sputter, comically feigning the expression of a man choking in noxious fumes. The muffled giggling that followed quickly drew the teacher's attention. When she turned around Max was still acting. So pointing to a per cent sign on the blackboard, she inquired icily, 'What does this mean Max?' There was no answer. Although Kevin was only laughing at Max along with the others now, his reputation as a troublemaker led the teacher to direct the same question to him. Again, there was no answer. She glowered at the three boys in the corner for a moment. Suspecting that Kevin and Carl were somehow mixed up in the disturbance, she finally announced: 'I am going to have a chat with you three boys after school.'[12]

In the second example, Mr. Geoffrey, a teacher, adopts his 'mock tiger stance', which his pupils have learned to define as amusing. He uses it when the going gets tough for them, where there has been a great effort by teacher and pupils, possibly accompanied, as in the following, by limited accomplishment:

11:22 'All for today. Put dictioinaries away. I have a little test for you. When you come into seventh grade you are supposed to know something: 2+2=4, C-a-t spells cat. Also should know states in your country.' Explains. Some dallying questions. Urges them 'Do your best. No excuses.' (LMS-sequence of influence attempts; comments before action rather than after.)[13]

11:25 Everyone starts. (LMS-this turns out to be quite difficult for these kids.) Much hesitancy. Questions back and forth among pupils. These are met with shrugs and subvocal 'I don't know'.

11:29 Geoffrey begins moving around and about. Collects from lunch girls.

11:34 'These maps of yours are miserable, stinking, terrible' [engaged in mock anger here]. (LMS-actually three or four states is about average. I was surprised at how poor the students were. Once again the limited knowledge.) 'Can't study history without knowing the states . . .' Pulls down map and has them start writing and copying them in. Brings out map game for them to use at leisure. 'At some time in next two weeks we will have a test for real.' Irma, with a horrified look, asks if it will go on their grade. As if there is something totally unfair about it.

11:38 Messenger. Cute little second grader. Geoffrey talks gently with her for a moment.

11:44 'How many have Mexico? TAKE IT OFF' (same as Canada).[14]

The preceding examples suggest that mental fatigue accumulates in those classrooms where pupils are not bored, but hard, often very hard, at work on something interesting enough to hold their attention. Boredom, as Woods has shown us, leads those students so afflicted to engage in antics, horseplay, wisecracks and other laughter-generating activities.[15] It takes root in an entirely different condition - namely, a lack of stimulation - rather than in so much stimulation that the mind pleads for a rest. Thus, it is possible that comic relief as a function of humour is most commonly observed in middle- and upper-class schools, when compared with inner-city schools attended by pupils from physically and educationally impoverished backgrounds or from culturally divergent ones.

Of the four functions of humour examined in this chapter, comic relief seems the one most squarely aimed at improving academic performance. It was found to help sustain concentration in theatre rehearsals, while the author's classroom research plus similar research by others suggest that humour can play the same role in school.[16] The other functions, at least as they have been observed to the present, relate chiefly to such issues as controlling disorderly behaviour, expressing personal animosity, and establishing rapport.

Nonetheless, the question of whether the use of comic relief promotes *greater* academic achievement than its nonuse (other things being equal) is complicated. The psychological evidence at hand indicates that humorous examples in lecture content result in no significant increase in comprehension when compared with lectures wanting in such content.[17] Recall is improved by the injection of humour, but it may be that only the humorous content is recalled better.

Yet, no research has been carried out directly on comic relief. In such research fatigue would have to be experimentally controlled and the humorous, and hence fatigue relieving, interjections of teachers *and* pupils identified and their effects noted. Even if it turned out, upon final analysis, that concentration sustained in this manner produced no significant increase in academic performance, the value of comic relief as a practice would probably still be confirmed. It is clearly more pleasant to do a task requiring a great deal of thinking when one feels up to it than when one is too tired. And, for most pupils, it must be more pleasant to be in school, whatever the grade, when they can have an occasional laugh and someone else is the butt of the humour.

Processes of Classroom Humour

At least four social psychological processes are present in intentional humour. One of these is the definition of the situation of the actor or humorist. Another is the definition of the same situation by the 'audience', or those that witness the humorous act, and the 'subject', butt, or target of the humour.[18] The third process is the humorist's presentation of self; the fourth is his or her role taking. All these processes, except the second, communicate some sort of information about the teacher's situated self.

Through the self presented by the humorist, the audience and subject learn something of the humorist's histrionic talents, skill in choosing words, ability to adopt linguistic accents, repertoire of jokes, imagination, and so forth. When the humour is deliberate, its content tells still more about the person from whom it came. In short, being purposely humorous informs others about that part of our personality related to our predisposition to humour and our ability to enact humour effectively.

From the humorist's standpoint defining the situation as calling for a humorous act is a process that takes place prior to that verbal or physical behaviour. There are at least four aspects to such a definition: mood, judgement, audience and subject. *Mood* refers to the emotional state of the humorist at the time of the humorous act. It may be affected by his or her *judgement* or appraisal of the nature of the activities of others in the setting. The nature of *audience* and *subject* is also established.

Mood, judgement, audience and subject, as they constitute the humorist's definition of the situation, determine the sociological function of a given humorous act in the larger social context. When the humorist's mood is lighthearted, the nature of the immediate activities judged to be genial, and the audience defined as friendly, the functional consequence is consensual humour. Subjects, in this instance, are variable. They may be disliked, tolerated, neutrally regarded, even liked or respected. A mood of apprehension, a judgement of threat, and a subject who is an antagonist together spawn control humour. The audience may be composed of friendly associates, other antagonists, uninvolved bystanders, or some other category of people or combination of categories. When conflict humour is enacted the humorist is hostile, judges the immediate activities with scorn, and sees the subject as some sort of enemy. Here, too, the audience, if there is one, may be variably defined. Finally, a serious mood combined with assiduous activity and an audience composed of one's colleagues or associates promotes humour that functions as comic relief. The subject may be from a wide variety of categories. These relationships are summarised in Table 4.1.[19]

It should be clear, however, that audience and subject may be the same person or persons and that humour may be subjectless. The latter condition is characteristic of many antics and witticisms. Further, the subject may be an abstract category, as in jokes about ethnic groups, stupid people, and farmers' daughters. Understandably, teachers are noticeably less apt to be subjects of humour than are one or more of their students, although there are exceptions, such as the self-deprecatory humour of a teacher observed by Waker and Goodson.[20]

Whether there is a subject to the humour and whether the humorist is teacher or pupil, appears to be related to the eventual function of the humour. The research in this area suggests that, when the teacher uses humour as an aggressive expression of hostility toward a pupil or group of pupils (conflict function) or as a means of controlling them, there is always a subject who is present in the classroom. The same holds when students

Table 2:
Humorist's Definition of the Situation
and Functional Consequences of His Intentional Humour

Mood	Judgement	Audience	Subject		Function
		Definition of the Situation			
Lighthearted	Genial	Friendly	Variable	→	Consensus
Apprehensive	Threatening	Variable	Antagonist	→	Control
Hostile	Scornful	Variable	Enemy	→	Conflict
Serious	Assiduous	Collegial	Variable	→	Comic relief

use humour to express aggression toward or to control their peers or, rarely the teacher. But the subject disappears or at least becomes general when the function of humour is consensual. Social cohesion in produced through the pleasant experience of laughing together at a joke, wisecrack, or antic. Audience (pupil) sympathy for one of their own who has been singled out as the butt of a joke would likely generate hostility and scorn for the teacher. The latter, however, could be the subject of clandestine consensual humour initiated by one of the pupils, as in the example of Mrs. Baxter presented later in this chapter.

In intentional humour the decision to be humorous must also include an estimate of the appropriateness of the humour for audience and subject. The humorist accomplishes this by taking the role of those affected, to determine their moods, judgements, and attitudes toward the proposed humour. In other words, subjects and audience also define the humorous situation and sometimes they define it as distinctly unamusing. Jokes may fall flat, antics are occasionally seen as childish, and funning is annoying at times. Successful humorists are sensitive to the feelings and views of their audiences and subjects and to the situations within which their humour is presented.

The social psychological processes of unintentional humour appear to be less complicated. Humorists become consciously involved only after the audience defines one of their spontaneous acts or utterances as amusing. One possible reaction to this public definition of their behaviour is embarrassment. The merriment that others find in the act in question is not genuinely shared by the reluctant humorist who has momentarily lost poise in the situation.

Forms of Classroom Humour

Whenever humour occurs people either intend to be funny or wind up being unintentionally funny. Either way the different forms of humour become sign vehicles for the presentation of self. My observations of classroom life suggest that the three forms of unintentional humour observed in other contexts - bloopers, stumbles, and accidents - also occur from time to time in classrooms.[21] If nothing else teachers can correct the immage that students might have of them as humourless, by allowing the pupils to have a laugh rather than trying to stifle this natural tendency. Moreover, unintentional humour has been observed to work to educational advantage by serving as a 'safety-valve' that helps reduce fatigue and boredom among students.[22]

The *blooper* is an involuntary wording blemish, such as an unwitting substitution of a word for the intended one, a reversal of two or more words, an omission of a key word, or a Freudian slip. *Stumbles* occur through involuntary stammering, or the momentary inability to enunciate a sentence as the speaker would like. The problem here is articulation rather than choice of words. An *accident* is any unintended act that evokes laughter from some or all of the others present in the classroom (e.g., dropping a tote tray, tripping over a chair leg). Peter Woods describes a humorous accident he had described to him in an English secondary school:

Dianne: What about when Mr. Bridge stood just outside the door.

Tracy: Dianne fell off a chair first and as she went to get up, she got 'old of me skirt, she was 'aving a muck about, and there was I in me petticoat, me skirt came down round my ankles and Mr. Bridge came in (*great screams of laughter from girls*). He'd been standing outside the door. . .[23]

To these three must be added a fourth form of unintentional humour, which is typical of classroom life. It is the *private joke*. In one version an utterance by the teacher tickles the funnybones of some of the students owing to the humorous connotations or associations it holds for them. In another, students are reminded through the teacher's talk of a joke or ludicrous incident they have shared, but of which the teacher is ignorant.

A teacher may also present aspects of self through intentional humour, which comes in a variety of forms: witticisms, antics, funning, practical jokes, narrative jokes, and sporting put-ons. *Witticisms* are ludicrous comments, which are expressed either as *put-downs* or *wisecracks*. The former is a degrading or severely critical comment; the latter is a clever remark or rejoinder and includes the pun. Among the wisecracks are the often imaginative nicknames students invent for the school staff.[24] Both the wisecrack and the put-down are illustrated in the following exchange between Mr. Simms, a teacher, and Stan, a tardy grade-eleven pupil.

> Students were arriving late that morning, as a result of a minor snowstorm that slowed the flow of traffic through the city. Mr. Simms, one of the high school mathematics teachers, said almost nothing to his latecomers, since he understood their problem that morning and since there were instructions from the Vice- Principal to admit them directly into class. But when Stan walked through the door thirty-five minutes after the period began, Mr. Simms waxed cynical. 'Why are we so honored this morning?' he inquired. Stan paused for a moment and then retorted: 'If you don't want me to come, I'll leave.' The class laughed. As he made his way to his desk, Mr.Simms made a further comment about the snow in Stan's driveway, and with more laughter from the rest of the students resumed the discussion of mathematical symbols.[25]

Antics are ludicrous gestures or acts. In the classroom nearly any behaviour can be construed as an antic: a comical face, a humorous posture, a funny motion with the hands or arms. Horseplay is perhaps the most common schoolhouse antic. The following incident observed by the author, though probably not classifiable as horseplay, is still typical of classroom antics:

> Mrs. Baxter was making the rounds to those of her pupils in need of help with the seatwork assignment. She taught in a traditional self-contained classroom, within which several ranks of desks were separated by aisles scarcely wide enough to allow student movement. Consequently, her rather portly frame, which nearly touched the desks on either side as she manoeuvred up the passageway, virtually pushed Anne, who was behind her, to the other side of her desk when she (the teacher) bent over to assist one of her classmates. For Anne the opportunity was irresistible. After quietly getting the attention of those nearby, she aimed a pair of compasses at the teacher's plump backsides, swung, and stopped within an inch of the unlikely target. Sniggering broke the studious quiet of the room. Annoyed, Mrs. Baxter whirled and scowled in the direction from which it came, though she had no idea of its cause.

Pupils, and sometimes even teachers, engage in *funning* or kidding within the schoolroom. In the interest of developing a set of mutually exclusive categories, it will refer here only to nondeceptive, albeit good-natured banter between pupils and teachers or among pupils exclusively. When deception is employed funning is more accurately treated as a variant of the sporting put-on. A close relative of funning is *practical joking* which, through some sort of trickery or abuse, places an individual at a disadvantage without introducing deception. Though teachers seldom condone them classroom examples are legion: putting tacks on chairs, firing rubber bands across the room, or stuffing grass clippings down someone's shirt. The practical joke contrasts with the *narrative joke* or the oral presentation of a brief humorous story.

Sporting put-ons refer to intentionally and successfully misleading acts (or products) engaged in for the fun they provide the deceiver.[26] Practical joking and funning that contain elements of deception, such as realistic rubber snakes and insects, squirting flowers, or taunts based on some fiction, fall into this category. Woods provides a combined example of a sporting put-on and funning:

> I witnessed another teacher having an elaborate game with the boys in one class focussed on the detection of cigarettes. 'Come on Dogsbody where are they, I know you've got some?' and searching a boy's clothing amidst jocular protests; finding some and confiscating them in mock triumph, only to return them with an indulgent grin at the end of the lesson.[27]

One reason for separating the sporting put-on from nondeceptive practical joking and funning is that being deceived frequently brings little pleasure to those who are made 'marks'. Rather they are embarrassed because their public images as reasonably perceptive and worldly-wise have been tarnished in some degree. Moreover, they may have lost a degree of respect for having been gullible, unsophisticated, or undiscriminating enough to be misled.

Conclusions

Using humour is like driving on a poorly maintained road; one does so at one's own risk. A practical joke may be carried off with the hope of generating amiability, but be defined by the subject as an aggressive, irritating act. Funning may turn into teasing where banter becomes ridicule. The would-be humorist must be aware of these hazards along the route to merriment.

Intentional humour can carry a variety of messages about school teachers' situated selves. Indeed, it can be one of the most poignant means of expression of their definitions of situations. Any form of humour with a subject or audience communicates the message that those people are worthy of some sort of attention, favourable or unfavourable. Humour that works to promote consensus indicates to the audience (and perhaps the subject) that they are worthy of sharing an atmosphere of good cheer with the humorist. Moreover, such humour tends to convey, albeit only temporarily, a degree of equality between humorist and audience. While they are laughing together at something, status differences are momentarily forgotten. In effect, humorist and audience are encouraged to interact by the former announcing his or her willingness to do so through the medium of genial humour. A joke or witticism, for example, also indicates that the humorist is at least in a cheerful mood, an affective state that pupils may sometimes be unable to discern in their teachers.

Teachers using humour to control their pupils convey a quite different message. For instance, when they humorously put down a pupil, they also call attention to teacher authority in the situated activity system of the classroom. At that point in time status differences are suddenly made to stand out in relief. Consequently, further interaction in the present is discouraged, since none of those involved is likely to be interested in associating with someone with whom they are on bad terms.

Humour constitutes a major type of sign vehicle, by means of which teachers correct misinformation or supplement a lack of information about themselves for their pupils. Effective interaction in any situated activity system, as Goffman notes, demands frequent adjustments of this sort. At the same time these humorous adjustments are also likely to be strategic in that they help establish consensus with, gain control over, engage in aggression toward, or provide comic relief for some or all of their pupils. But the possible misapplication of humour must also be guarded against, for it can harden relations with them.

Endnotes

1. Peter Woods, 'Having a Laugh: an Antidote to Schooling' in M. Hammersley and P. Woods (eds.), The Process of Schooling (Routledge and Kegan Paul, London, 1976), pp. 178—87; Roy Nash, 'Pupil's Expectations of Their Teachers', in M. Stubbs and S. Delamont (eds.), Explorations in Classroom Observation (John Wiley, London, 1976), pp. 83—98.

2. For example, see Willard Waller, The Sociology of Teaching (John Wiley, New York, 1932), pp. 229—30.

3. For example, see M. Dale Baughman, 'Joy in the Junior and Middle School', NASSP Bulletin, 57 (1973), pp. 51—9; Hap Gilliland and Harriett Mauritsen, 'Humor in the Classroom', Reading Teacher, 24 (1971), pp. 753—6; Gunnar Horn, 'Laughter: a Saving Grace', Today's Education, 61 (1972), pp.37—8.

4. Erving Goffman, Encounters: (Bobbs-MerrIll, Indianapolis, 1961), pp.95—9.

5. Ibid., pp. 99—105.

6. Louis M. Smith and William Geoffrey, The Complexities of an Urban Classroom (Holt, Rinehart and Winston, New York, 1968); Ronald G. Corwin, A Sociology of Education (Appleton-Century-Crofts, New York, 1965). pp. 301, 320—26: Nash. 'Pupil's Expectations of Their Teachers': Woods. 'Having a Laugh': Rob Walker and Clem Adelman, 'Strawberries', in M. Stubbs and S. Delamont (eds.), Explorations in Classroom Observation (John Wiley. London, 1976), pp. 133–50: Rob Walker and lvor Goodson, 'Humour in the Classroom', in P. Woods and M. Hammersley' (eds.). School Experience (Croom Helm, London. 1977), pp. 196—227: P. Woods, The Divided School (Routledge' and Kegan Paul, London, 1979).

7. William H. Martineau, 'A Model of the Social Functions of Humor', in J. H. Goldstein and P.E. McGhee (eds.). The Psychology of Humor (Academic Press, New York, 1972), pp. 103—14.

8. On aggression in general, see Arnold H. Buss, 'Physical Aggression in Relation to Different Frustrations', Journal of Abnormal and Social Psychology, 67 (1963), pp. 1—7.

9. Robert A. Stebbins, 'Comic Relief in Everyday Life: Dramaturgic Observations on a Function of Humor', Symbolic Interaction, forthcoming.

10. Clifford T. Morgan and Richard A. King, Introduction to Psychology, 4th ed. (McGraw-Hlll, New York. 1971), pp. 565—9.

11. See Robert A. Stebbins, The Disorderly Classroom: Its Physical and Temporal Conditions, Monographs in Education No. 12 (Faculty of Education, Memorial University, St. John's, Newfoundland, 1974).

12. Robert A. Stebbins, Teachers and Meaning: Definitions of Classroom Situations (E.J. Brill, Leiden, 1975), p. 67.

13. LMS is Louis Smith, the participant observer and co-author of the book from which this passage is taken.

14. Smith and Geoffrey. The Complexities of an Urban Classroom, p. 207.

15. Woods. 'Having a Laugh', p. 181.

16. Stebbins. 'Comic Relief in Everyday Life'.

17. See, for example, Robert M. Kaplan and Gregory C. Pascoe, 'Humorous Lectures and Humorous Examples', Journal of Educational Psychology, 69 (1977), pp. 61—5; Dorothy Markiewicz, 'Effects of Humor on Persuasion', Sociometry. 37 (1974), pp. 407—22; William E. Hauck and John W. Thomas, 'Relationship of Humor to Intelligence, Creativity, and Intentional and Incidental Learning', Journal of Experimental Education, 40 (1972), pp. 52—5.

18. Martineau. 'A Model of the Social Functions of Humor', 114.

19. It should be clear that I am speaking of system maintaining functions. But, even here, the functional consequences may occasionally be more complicated than Table 2 suggests. For example, conflict humour whose subject is outside the classroom could have the effect of generating solidarity within it, as teacher and pupils laugh together. Thus, it also functions as consensual humour.

20. Walker and Goodson, 'Humour in the Classroom', pp. 203—8.

21. The observations of classroom life are reported in Robert A. Stebbins. The Disorderly Classroom; Teachers and Meaning. On unintentional humour see Robert A. Stebbins, 'Comic Relief in Everyday Life'.

22. Stebbins, The Disorderly Classroom, pp. 51, 58—60.

23. Woods, 'Having a Laugh', p. 178.

24. See Woods, ibid., p. 184; Waller, Sociology of Teaching, p. 349.

25. Stebbins, Teachers and Meaning, p. 113.

26. Robert A. Stebbins, 'Putting People on: Deception of our Fellowman in Everyday Life', Sociology and Social Research, 59 (1975), pp. 189—200.

27. Woods, 'Having a Laugh', p. 183.

Chapter 9

ALONENESS*

I did live, as I said, with one person for a long time. And I loved that communion and that routine and that coming together in the evening and having a drink and talking. This is very precious. I miss it. I am terribly lonely now, but I have also become enamoured of solitude. That's my last great love.

My solitude is everywhere and sometimes I don't speak to anyone, except just to say good morning to the post mistress, for days, for days literally in the winter. And this is hard to handle, to not get unbalanced and not let depression get hold of you. Everything becomes more intense, you see, which is partly why it's marvelous. There's nothing to break the intensity. the great flow from the subconscious to the conscious is the good thing about solitude. There is no barrier between the subconscious and the conscious, or much less than there is if you are talking to a person, when you are constantly taking them into account, especially if you love people as I do. (May Sarton. *A Self-Portrait*, edited by Marita Simpson and Martha Whellock. New York: W.W. Norton, 1988, p. 22.)

The significance of aloneness or solitude has not been missed down through history, even if modern social science has failed to give it attention. Cicero, for instance, observed that one is "never less idle than when wholly idle, nor less alone than when wholly alone." Rousseau was more specific in his appraisal: "Never have I thought so much, existed so much, lived so much, been so much myself, if I may dare to say it, as when I went alone and afoot." For Wordsworth aloneness was a sort of retreat:

*Aloneness: A neglected condition. Paper presented at the Annual Meeting of the American Sociological Association, New York, August, 1976.

When from our better selves we have too long

Been parted by the hurrying world, and droop,

Sick of its business, of its pleasures tired,

How gracious, how benign, is Solitude.

Thoreau whose penchant for aloneness is well known stressed another source of this condition:

> I never found the companion that was so companionable as solitude. We are for the most part more lonely when we go abroad among men than when we stay in our chanbers. A man thinking or working is always alone, let him be where he will.

Thoreau could have had Benjamin Franklin in mind, for the latter also knew the value of solitude as indicated in his adage: "He may well win the face that runs by himself."

That so many prominent figures have found it worth their time to comment on one aspect or another of aloneness suggests that social science ought to take a serious look at it too. As a start toward its scientific study, aloneness may be defined as freedom from the demands of interaction with other people and from the interruptions and distractions caused by their activities while pursuing some personal interest or concern. Both Americans and American social scientists tend to stress its opposite - gregariousness - as the more desirable state and, apparently, as the more worthy of examination. The Bible encourages this orientation by reporting God's observation that "It is not good that man should be alone; I will make an help meet for him." The result was Eve. Today other-directed men spurn their less common inner-directed brothers in part because those brothers are loners (Reisman, 1961:155), whereas the "independent spirits' among us are lauded in part because they are able to withstand the so-called pathos of aloneness (Klapp, 1972:43). Some respondents in the present study admitted to holding a similar outlook on voluntary solitude, even while also admitting they frequently seek it (see later). Social scientists agree that human beings are strongly motivated to interact with one another (Abrahamson, 1966:148; Sullivan, 1953:270-71, 370).

Aloneness may be understood as one form of *seclusion*. On occasion, a handful of scholars have attended to two other forms closely related to it; namely, privacy and loneliness. Since the similarities and differences between these two and aloneness have never been explored, this becomes the first task of this paper. Once this is accomplished we turn to its main purpose: the presentation of an exploratory study of aloneness.

Aloneness, Privacy, and Loneliness

Privacy is the withdrawal or shielding from observation by others (through any of their senses) of one's person, behavior, thoughts, or property (on the privacy of property, see Heider, 1958:62; Manning, 1972:83-94). Lopata (1969:249) defines loneliness as:

A sentiment felt by a person when he defines his experienced level or form of interaction as inadequate. Such feelings are likely to arise when the habitual or expeted depth of relations with other people is judged as temporarily or permanently unavailable, broken, or underdeveloped.

As these definitions and the earlier one of aloneness indicate, both objective and subjective sides exist on the description and analysis of seclusion. Objectively particular conditions in social life typically accompany its various forms such as a shielding of something, a freedom from interaction with others, or a break in or unavailability of interpersonal relationships.

Subjectively people *define* certain situations as characterized by one of these three types of conditions (on the subjective structure of privacy, see Bates, 1964:430-31). They believe they are experiencing, have experienced, or will experience aloneness, privacy, or loneliness. In addition to being a condition of social life loneliness, because it is abhorred, and at times even feared, is a sentiment of the lonely.

Aloneness, privacy, and loneliness may occur in absolute seclusion from or in the presence of certain other people (relative seclusion). The seclusivenss of a situation identified as one of these three is very much a matter of interpretation by the secluded person. In aloneness, for example, one may seek the absolute solitude of a study to contemplate certain alternatives in one's occupational career or the relative aloneness of a crowd of shoppers to escape family pressures momentarily. Both Bates (1964:430) and Schwartz (1968:742-43) have indicated that privacy entails restricting observation for *some* but not necessarily all people. "The general rule. . .," says Schwartz (1968:743), "is that outside the kinship group an extreme rank is conferred upon those for whom privacy shields are voluntarily removed." Turning to loneliness, Lopata (1969) and Moustakas (1961) both note that this state occurs in the presence of others.

People often feel lonely for a person, object, event, interaction scene, or mood which had been experienced in the past. . . . A person may feel lonely when no one else is present, when a particular partner is absent, when interaction partners treat him differently than he desires. . . (Lopata, 1969:250).

Simmel (1902:36) concluded that loneliness is seldom more poignant than when one is a stranger and without attachments among many physically adjacent people.[1]

Because of these similarities aloneness, privacy, and loneliness are best differentiated by their antecedent motivational states. That is, both privacy and aloneness are purposeful. But only privacy is *protective*; it being sought or welcomed in an attempt to avoid observation of self, behavior, thought, or property. A secret is actually shielded, or at least believed to be shielded, from someone else; we have "information preserves," access to which we control while in the presence of others (Goffman, 1971:38-40). The final section of this paper shows how the concepts of privacy and aloneness are frequently confused by referring to the latter in the name of the former.

By contrast, aloneness is *facilitative*. Being free from the necessity of interaction with others and from their distracting and interrupting activities, the individual is able to pursue his or her personal interest or concern. Further, comments by many of the respondents suggest that aloneness is a scarce value of which they would like to have more. This is especially true for housewives with small children - they vigorously seek it. Others, knowing that their daily or weekly schedule will eventually afford them sufficient solitude, simply wait for it to occur rather than adjust their agendas to fit it in. Perhaps in response to our cultural de-emphasis on aloneness, some of these same people worry about incurring too much of it or being considered odd for desiring it. Although mutualy exclusive, privacy and aloneness can characterize the same situation in that protective *and* facilitative motives propel the activity of the moment.

Loneliness, on the one hand, is an *unmotivated* and *unwanted* condition or situation produced by a set of antecedent circumstances beyond the individual's control. On the other hand, it is also a sentiment that begets motives, chiefly to overcome, reduce, or avoid the agony of involuntary seclusion.

It follows from what has been said so far that it is inaccurate to speak of excess privacy (as do Schwartz, 1968:751 and Bates, 1964:431) or excess aloneness (as did a few respondents in the present study), for subjectively such a thing is impossible since they are purposeful. Moreover such excess can never lead to loneliness, as these same authors contend. Because we have no continuum here, privacy and aloneness are more or less within the person's control, whereas he or she is largely powerless against loneliness.

Types of Aloneness

Frieda Fromm-Reichmann is possibly the only social scientist to identify aloneness as a singular condition. Nonetheless her principal interest is in "destructive" or "real loneliness," which she separates from several similar conditions included by Moustakas and Lopata in their broader discussion of loneliness (Fromm-Reichmann, 1959:2). Important for our purposes is her treatment of "self-imposed loneliness" as clearly distinct from other kinds of loneliness, especially the destructive kind. That treatment is brief, however, and consequently fails to do justice to the complexity and uniqueness of aloneness as a form of seclusion.

Moustakas (1961:43) discusses a special form of loneliness that emerges as a happy, benign sequel to the pathetic experience of destructive loneliness, a sequel leading ultimately to creative contributions in art, literature, and science. He also says:

> Rather than separating the individual or causing a break or division of self, [benign loneliness] expands the individual's wholeness, perceptiveness, sensitivity, and humanity. It enables the person to realize human ties and awareness hitherto unknown (Moustakas,1971:47).[2]

If this be aloneness it is hardly the usual, self-imposed or purposeful variety on which the present paper focuses, although we shall note some similarities later.

With so little previous research or thought to go on, the first need is to discover the types of aloneness and the conditions facilitating and hindering them. This groundwork will enable a brief look at the significance of aloneness, which is saved for the concluding section of this paper.

Preliminary discussions with individual students and colleagues suggested three types of aloneness: (1) aloneness to accomplish a task or reach a goal; (2) aloneness to relax while away from people; (3) aloneness to think about past, present, and future problems and events involving ourselves and others. With this background ninety-eight upper-division university students were asked to write anonymously up to three recent examples from their lives of each of these three types. At the end of the survey form they were further invited to express their additional thoughts on aloneness that could be of use in the study and to indicate if they had too much or too little aloneness. From these unstructured comments a fourth type of aloneness emerged, namely, solitude in order to commune with the Deity. These four types are referred to from here on as *goal-oriented, relaxation, contemplative,* and *religious* aloneness, respectively.

For every example they recorded the respondents were asked to describe what they did while alone, where they did it, how long it took, and what sort of interruptions or distractions they experienced, if any. Certain face-sheet data were collected as well.

Goal-oriented Aloneness

Four subtypes of goal-oriented aloneness emerged from the examples. In two of them the person is mastering or manipulating ideas: aloneness to *study and learn* and aloneness to complete or continue work on a *project*. The projects are of endless variety. The respondents seek or welcome solitude when planning a budget, writing a report or paper, planning their daily or weekly schedules, preparing a Sunday School lesson, writing a letter, designing a pamphlet, organizing a club, and the like. The remaining two subtypes center on physical rather than mental concerns: aloneness is sought or welcomed to do a *task* and to perfect or express a *physical skill*. Among the tasks mentioned were fixing an automobile exhaust leak, repairing something at home, cleaning house, paying a bill, and running an errand. The skills expressed or practiced while alone include sewing, playing a musical instrument, doing a dance step, and swimming for form.

We turn first to certain demographic correlates. Men are somewhat more likely than women to work alone on projects. Yet comments made by the women imply that, as a group, they seem to value aloneness more than men do, probably owing to the bothersome presence of children for some of them. Mens' projects more often take them away from their families to the seclusion of workshops or out-of-doors to their automobiles. That single respondents reported considerably more solitary expression or perfection of a skill than married respondents probably reflects the fact of decreased privacy in marriage. At least this finding cannot be traced to a lack of company at home among single respondents, for all but two lived with one or more adults.

Everyone in the sample who had skills to perfect seemed to want aloneness for this purpose. All the respondents commented on how the process of refining a skill may be physically awkward or aurally noxious, efforts the person would as soon keep hidden from others and that he or she probably rightly suspects they would as soon not witness. Some described how they talk to themselves while alone for this purpose and otherwise behave in ways conducive to embarrassment were outsiders to look in on the proceedings. Finally, the perfection of skills requires concentration, which is facilitated by solitude.[3]

Relaxation Aloneness

It was possible to identify six major subtypes of relaxation aloneness from among approximately the same number of examples as presented by the respondents for goal-oriented aloneness. In their solitude they *relax at home* by engaging in a variety of activities: for instance, sewing, singing, reading, gardening, writing poetry, shooting baskets (in basketball), embroidering, playing a musical instrument, taking a bath, washing hair, and cooking or baking. The respondents also relax more or less passively at home, by sitting, suntanning, listening to the radio or phonograph, watching television, lying in bed, or sitting in the bathtub. Third, these people *relax alone in public places* in an active fashion. Among other things, they eat in restaurants, drive cars or ride bicycles or motorcycles (in town), walk dogs, go shopping, stroll or run along the street, swim in a pool, read in the parks or elsewhere, and play guitars. There are also passive ways of relaxing alone in public: for example, one may window-shop, sit in a parked car, sit in a park or some other public place, or suntan at a public beach.

Fifth, some respondents *relax in the solitude of natural settings* through such activities as canoeing, sailing, rowing, swimming, hiking, fishing, hunting, and horseback riding. One woman who enjoys solitary motorcycling across the country, commented:

> I am preoccupied with the road when I am driving, but when I stop in an isolated spot, there is a joy that comes over me - an isolated awareness of self, and I know I am a creature of worth. There is a freedom and it's mine (reported in Korsak, 1975).

Others choose passive, solitary relaxation in these surroundings, usually just sitting. A small number mentioned a seventh subtype: passive *relaxation at their place of work* such as lounging behind a closed office door. Whatever the subtype of relaxation aloneness, drinking or smoking something was often regarded as a vital part of the activity because it contributes directly to the relaxation.

For some in the sample relaxation aloneness is unimportant, or less important than the other types. Seven respondents said they prefer to relax with their spouse or a close friend rather than alone. Four said they have no chance to relax alone, which they seemed not to miss. The majority, however, desire and obtain relaxation alone at particular times and relaxation in certain company at other times. The wish for companionship depends on the purpose of the relaxation. Some respondents explicitly stated that they relax to relieve tension accumulated over the preceding hours. Here company, assuming it produces little or no additional stress, may be welcome.[4]

Still, other respondents say they tire from the sort of alertness demanded for satisfactory social interaction. Such weariness is explained by the observation that experience must flow in interchanges with others (Matza, 1969:122). Awkward pauses in interaction lead to embarrassment and confusion even though the actors intend no such consequences, and their true aims may be misperceived as they silently rest. Daydreaming in the midst of a conversation, although relaxing for the dreamer, is likely to be considered rude by other people. The safest strategy is to retreat momentarily from *all* people. Nevertheless we frequently try to relax between scheduled events, although we may have no choice, whatever our preference, but to accept company, there being no refuge available for solitary relaxation.

Some forms of relaxation such as bathing, generally leave the respondents with no alternative - should they even want it - but to engage in them alone. the studies of privacy and aloneness converge, among other places, in the seclusion sought for this sort of activity and that sought for certain deviant activities (see Schwartz, 1968:744-45). All socially unacceptable habits and certain illegal practices pursued as recreation are best kept concealed from everyone. No information was gathered from the sample on these subjects, but it is noteworthy that the reading of pornographic books has been found to be a solitary pastime for about half the adolescents interviewed for another study (Commission on Obscenity and Pornography, 1970:156).

At least for the respondents in the present study, home is clearly the preferred setting for relaxation aloneness when compared with public places and natural surroundings. Further, the married use public places for active, solitary relaxation more than the single do. This pattern may be due to a lack of privacy at home or to the fact that some kinds of relaxation solitude are possible only in nondomestic settings. To a degree women also engage more than men in passive, solitary relaxation in public, as typically manifested in window-shopping or lying in the sun.[5]

Contemplative Aloneness

Eight subtypes of contemplative aloneness were abstracted from the respondents' examples. The two most prevalent are aloneness to consider the past, present, and future of one's *occupational or educational career*; and aloneness to think through, from one of these time perspectives, *interpersonal problems* (e.g., a disagreement, a mutual decision) involving relatives, friends, spouse, or work associates. The large number of examples classified as "*personal problems* (not elsewhere included)" is possibly inaccurate. Individual problems such as bad habits (e.g., smoking, drunkenness), financial difficulties, or prospective major purchases (e.g., house, car), were placed here. Several respondents, however, simply wrote about personal problems with no precise indication of their nature. These examples were also coded in this category, although some of them could actually have been interpersonal or occupational career problems. Owing to the uncertainty about these data, aloneness to consider personal problems is omitted from further consideration.

The remaining less frequent subtypes emerging from the analysis included: aloneness to think about the past, present, or future of important *interpersonal relationships* (e.g., spouse, boyfriend, girlfriend, fiance[e], close friend); aloneness to consider one's *life career or biography*, which sometimes embraces such lofty speculation as one's place in the universe; past oriented aloneness to *reminisce* about former interpersonal relationships and events; often while listening to recorded music. A sizeable number of the examples focused on the *problems of others*. A much smaller number were concerned with past and present *social problems* or major current events, local and extralocal.

The idea of subjective career is central to three of these subtypes. Subjective career is "the actor's recognition and interpretation of past and future events associated with a particular identity, and especially his interpretationion of important contingencies as they were or will be encountered" (Stebbins, 1970:34). The respondents' examples showed how uninterrupted aloneness is used to ponder career commitments and attachments, conflicts within and between those careers, overall strategies for achieving success in them, and the like. The examples also showed how crucial problems and events are defined prospectively, retrospectively, and conditionally (see Znaniecki, 1952:251; Stebbins, 1975:25-26).[6] In thinking about others' problems, it is evident from the examples that what Znaniecki called "vicarious" definitions of the situation are often constructed as well. In short contemplative aloneness, since it is sometimes used to consider personal careers of one sort or another, helps establish continuity or integration in the lives of those who engage in it.

Finding a time and place for contemplative aloneness can be a problem. Many respondents want to reflect about a major event as soon after its occurrence as possible. As the aloneness needed to do this may be impossible to find just then, reflection is postponed. This predicament helps explain the attractiveness of the bathtub and shower for problem-solving contemplation. More common, however, is thinking in bed before falling asleep or in some other part of the house after others have retired for the night. In the meantime, but especially just after the event, behavior and thought connected with less significant matters are no doubt impeded by the individual's preoccupation with its meaning.

A handful of respondents (fewer than in relaxation aloneness) said they preferred to talk over their career (occupational, life, interpersonal relationship) and personal problems with one other special peson such as a spouse or close friend. This is the exception, however, not the rule. Career and personal problems can be vexatious and complex with solutions having distant consequences. The individual is understandably wont to attend exclusively to their many details. As previously noted social intercourse suffers when people disengage themselves for such purposes; others who are present react with confusion and embarrassment. So absolute solitude at some point is the ideal context for most respondents facing momentous decisions. For affectively charged problems and events we are aided by the customary seclusion granted us when recovering from or in the throes of intense emotional experiences (Bates, 1964:431).[7]

Times and places for absolute aloneness are scarce. This may partly account for the small number of examples of contemplative aloneness (some respondents listed none at all) in contrast to the large number of examples of goal-oriented and relaxation aloneness. But the number of examples of each type of aloneness can also be interpreted as a reflection of the actual need the respondents have for it. People may have greater need for aloneness to finish tasks, reach goals, and relax, than to muse about their few serious personal and career problems. There is individual variation here, nonetheless, for a small percentage of respondents reported engaging in a great deal of contemplative aloneness.

Some important sex and marital differences emerged. First men, when pondering their life careers, engage in noticeably more contemplative aloneness than women. Second single, when compared with married, respondents show a marked tendency to seek or welcome aloneness as the setting for thought about interpersonal relationships, usually serious bonds with members of the opposite sex. The respondents who offered these examples, however, all lived with at least one other adult, the mode being two. This finding suggests that aloneness is a style of confronting the problems of relationship choice and development especially typical of young people (all were twenty-five years of age or under) whose ties with the opposite sex are still transient.

Third, single men and women, usually twenty years old or younger, used aloneness to relive special memories. Again this solitude is not due to isolation, but to a preference for it when reminiscing. Fourth, married respondents are noticeably more likely than single ones to seek or welcome aloneness for dealing with interpersonal problems. This tendency is probaby best explained by the self-evident condition that to have a spouse (many respondents had no children) merely puts one in a position of having more interpersonal problems with which to cope. A fifth difference is the marked tendency for people in the age category of twenty-one to twenty-five years to consider their present and future occupational and education careers in solitude. These respondents, too, lived with at least one other adult. That they are deliberating on their plans and progress in school and work should come as no surprise, given their age. It is their use of aloneness that is of interest.[8]

Religious Aloneness

Religious aloneness normally takes the form of prayer, either at home or at a religious institution or at both. The small number of respondents who cited this type of solitude failed to specify if they pray sporadically about a particular problem - a variant of contemplative aloneness - or routinely often without reference to specific difficulties in their lives. Since some people pray regularly and alone, whether they face crucial problems or not, a separate category of solitude is justified. Still, communion with God, when done at a house of worship, is at times only relative aloneness, for others who are engaging in the same behavior may be present.

Interruptions and Distractions

The vast majority of respondents resented interruptions and distractions of their aloneness. An interruption or the termination of a session of aloneness for the time being is initiated by other people, by unavoidable scheduled events, by physiological demands, and by personal thoughts. The telephone and physical intrusions by friends, relatives, spouses, and work associates are the two primary ways other people interrupt solitude whatever its type. Scheduled events of all sorts may have the same effect, as in a call to dinner, an appointment somewhere, a class that is about to start, and so on. Such "physiological time demands" (Moore, 1963:15) as the need for sleep or food were occasionally reported as arresting aloneness. Even daydreams or a wondering mind may halt it. A daydream may end contemplation about a personal problem; a wondering mind may alert us to an unfilled obligation.

A distraction halts or disturbs solitary activity, but only temporarily; the session of aloneness may well continue afterward. Other people provide many of the respondents' distractions by coming into the space where solitude is taking place or by calling on the telephone, although engaging them only briefly. In these instances the person is forced into social interaction. In other instances aloneness may be indirectly distracted by activities or sounds in the same space or adjacent ones, most likely voices from another room, music heard through a wall, or noises from animals (chiefly dogs). Even pets may distract by demanding attention. Many respondents stated that interruptions and distractions are resented more when they impinge upon goal-oriented and contemplative aloneness than upon relaxation aloneness.

Because we expect interruptions and distractions of our aloneness, we take precautions to avoid them. One strategy is to inform others that we wish to be left undisturbed, as by withdrawing to a bedroom and shutting the door (on the importance of doors in privacy, see Schwartz, 1968:747-49). Some respondents schedule periods of aloneness at times when they know they can avoid interruptions or distractions. Hence the frequency of aloneness at night after some or all other membes of the household have gone to bed. Culturally defined spaces for aloneness also exist, often being the same ones as for privacy (Schwartz, 1968:745-51). Here rules forbid disturbing the users of such places as libraries, bedrooms, bathrooms, and houses of worship; if we want solitude we may head for one of these sanctuaries.

If there were no interruptions how long would aloneness last? The ultimate answer to this question must be partly based on the reasons for seeking or welcoming seclusion. All we can say at this primitive stage in the study of aloneness is that, in the examples reported, solitude lasted from a few minutes to several days, the latter only in the wilderness.

Significance of Aloneness

Some fascinating research questions await our consideration in the study of aloneness. Data from investigations of loneliness and from the present exploration suggest that the desire for aloneness varies with age and possibly marital status. The aged, for instance, crave companionship but find it lacking; loneliness is a major problem for them (e.g., Lopata, 1969; Seabrook, 1973). There may be situations in which aloneness is particularly prized because it is so difficult to find there. Inmates in total institutions of every kind encounter this deficiency.

> Besides the loss of freedom, besides the forced labor, there is another torture in prison life, almost more terrible than any other - that is compulsory life in common.

> I could never have imagined, for instance, how terrible and agonizing it would be never once for a single minute to be alone for the ten years of my imprisonment (Dostoevsky, *The House of the Dead*).

The quest for solitude and its availability may also vary by social class. At least such variation has been observed for privacy (Goffman, 1971:40-41). The importance of aloneness in marriage has already been to some extent in the popular press under the heading of "privacy" (O'Neill and O'Neill, 1972:86-96). Nor should we ignore the hints, given us by the respondents, of the role played by space in fostering or inhibiting solitude. Sommer (1969: ch. 4) touches on this theme in his discussion of crowding and privacy.

What of the broader implications of the practice of individual aloneness? The value of the study of aloneness for social science goes well beyond the mere description of some seemingly antisocial curiosity heretofore overlooked. First, like privacy (Schwartz, 1968:741), aloneness serves community integration through separation. Concerted social life would become most precarious were members of society, because of insufficient opportunities for solitude, unable to achieve those goals associated with the division of labor. Aloneness and privacy as highly institutionalized forms of withdrawal help preserve the group by enabling people to carry out tasks requiring solitude.

Second, relations with others are likely to be smoother to the extent that, as individuals, we are personally integrated. Rousseau's comment earlier in this paper suggests this. Or, in the words of one respondent:

> I feel that I personally have an innate need to be alone at least a percentage of the time. It is as natural as sleep, and when deprived of aloneness I am irritated, frustrated, and fail to function at a satisfactory level of accomplishment. I think aloneness is essential to understanding one's self and a necessity for performing even daily tasks efficiently.

Aloneness facilitates contemplation of the past, present, and future of our principal role identities; continuity of self is established in this manner.

Third, and most significant, all types of aloneness allow adjustment to the pressures and obligations of daily living. It is this function that the data reported here demonstrate best. In our solitude we finish projects, make plans, and rehearse skills; we nurse social wounds, redefine important events, and solve personal problems, we retreat from the demands of interhuman association where we rest our bodies, calm our anxieties, and rejuvenate our social skills for the next entrance into public life. Plant noted this function of aloneness over forty years ago, without however dwelling on the concept as such:

[we face] the mental strain arising from constantly having to "get along" with other people.... In the strain of having constantly to adapt to others there is a continuous challenge to the integrity of [the child's defenses], and the child gives to us beautifully the irritable, restless, insecure picture which proclaims this everpresent threat. Often adults feel the strain of having to adjust to others if they are persistently in a group for a period of time. We see children who have never known any other situation (Plant, 1930:853).

Those who seek or welcome aloneness from time to time are not loners. With a few exceptions the respondents surveyed appeared to be gregarious enough to avoid the stigma of excessive inner-direction. Yet precisely because we live in an other-directed community, aloneness is prominent as a mode of adjustment in everyday life and hence a proper subject for social scientific scrutiny.

Endnotes

1. "Loneliness anxiety" – loneliness experienced in connection with the future as, for example in the fear of losing a beloved companion – is excluded from the present discussion. Nonetheless it is a characteristic of some loneliness which helps distinguish loneliness from privacy and aloneness.

2. Sullivan's (1953:270–71) work in this area suggests that this sort of transformation of the psychological impact of destructive loneliness is only partial. Weiss (1973:14) appears to support his observations.

3. Additional although indirect support comes from research on social facilitation, which suggests that audiences may decrease effectiveness in tasks requiring concentration (Shaw, 1971:59).

4. One respondent said he preferred to spend all his time with the girl to whom he is engaged. The relationship is too exciting at this point to search for isolation from the partner.

5. It was impossible to neatly classify every example of solitude as either of the goal-oriented or of the relaxation type. A few respondents reported that taking a bath, practicing a musical instrument or making something alone are, for them, both ends to be achieved and means of relaxation. Rather than exclude them from the analysis, examples of this kind were alternately sorted, as they came to my attention, into one or the other of these two types of aloneness. Other respondents gave examples of

goal-oriented aloneness followed by relaxation aloneness within the same period of continuous solitude. Sometimes these activities were difficult to separate as when one person sat down to read a magazine article (goal-oriented), finished it, and started immediately on a short story in the same periodical (relaxation). With some effort, nevertheless, examples of this nature could be unambiguously classified.

The empirical problem of phenomenological overlap among the respondents in their placement of their own examples of aloneness must also be confronted. Sewing (not mending) is exclusively goal-oriented aloneness for one individual while it is exclusively relaxation aloneness for another. Again the importance of considering the subjective outlook on aloneness is evident. One behavioral means of distinguishing the type of solitude being reported (unless it is a mixture of types) is to establish how the subject pursues it. Relaxation activities should, in general, be casual, easeful, and unhurried, whereas goal-oriented activities should be more serious, tense, and urgent, although not necessarily to the point of frenzy and loss of control.

6. Lindsmith et al. (1975:456) comment on the importance of privacy in such reflective activity.

7. Generally we seek aloneness to contemplate important problems and events, even to the exclusion of significant others. But those same others may be quickly consulted to determine their opinion once a tentative solution or conclusion has been reached in seclusion.

8. In analyzing contemplative aloneness, as in analyzing the other types, examples turned up that fit imperfectly. Some respondents reported mixing solitary relaxation with contemplation on a particular problem or event. Others said they worked alone at a goal during which time they also mulled over a bothersome matter. Although no examples were reported, it is also possible for one contemplation on problems and events to follow or precede aloneness for other ends. Yet, at bottom, contemplative aloneness is distinct. It is unlikely to be defined under other circumstances as goal-oriented or relaxation aloneness.

References

Abrahamson, M.
  1966 *Interpersonal Accommodation.* D. Van Nostrand.

Bates, A.P.
  1964 Privacy: A Useful Concept? *Social Forces* 42:429-434.
         Commission on Obscenity and Pornography. 1970. *Report of the Commission on Obscenity and Pornography.* Bantom Books.

Fromm-Reichmann, F.
  1959 Loneliness. *Psychiatry* 22:1-16.

Goffman, E. 1971. *Relations in Public.* Harper & Row.

Heider, F.
  1948 *The Psychology of Interpersonal Relations.* John Wiley.

Klapp, O. E.
  1972 *Heroes, Villans, and Fools.* Aegis.

Korsak, F.
  1975 Cycling Free. *Dallas Times Herald.* Tuesday, July 1.

Lindesmith, A.R., Strauss, A.L., & Denzin, N.
  1975 *Social Psychology*, 4th ed. Dryden.

Lopata, H.Z.
  1969 Loneliness: Forms and Components. *Social Problems* 17:248-262.

Manning, P.K.
  1972 Locks and Keys: An Essay on Privacy. In J.M. Henslin (ed.), *Down to Earth Sociology.* Free Press.

Matza, D.
  1969 *Becoming Deviant.* Prentice-Hall.

Moore, W.E.
  1963 *Man, Time, and Society.* John Wiley.

Moustakas, C.E.
  1961 *Loneliness.* Prentice-Hall.

O'Neill, N., and O'Neill, G.
   1972 *Open Marriage*. Avon.

Plant, J.
   1930 Some Psychiatric Aspects of Crowded Living Conditions. American Journal of Psychiatry 5:849-860.

Reisman, D.
   1961 *The Lonely Crowd*, abridged ed. Yale University Press.

Schwartz, B.
   1968 The Social Psychology of Privacy. *American Journal of Sociology* 73:741-752.

Seabrook, J.
   1973 *Loneliness*. Maurice Temple Smith.

Shaw, M.E.
   1971 *Group Dynamics*. McGraw-Hill.

Simmel, G.
   1902 The Number of Members as Determining the Sociological Form of the Group. *American Journal of Sociology* 8:1-46.

Sommer, R.
   1969 *Personal Space*. Prentice-Hall.

Stebbins, R.
   1970 Career: The Subjective Approach. *Sociological Quarterly* 11:32-49.

Stebbins, R.
   1975 *Teachers and Meaning: Definitions of Classroom Situations*. E. J. Brill.

Sullivan, H.S.
   1953 *The Interpersonal Theory of Psychiatry*. W. W. Norton.

Weiss, R.S., (ed.).
   1973 *Loneliness*. M.I.T. Press.

Znaniecki, F.
   1952 *Cultural Sciences*. University of Illinois Press.

Chapter 10

CONCLUSION

> In one sense this secular world is not so irreligious as we might think. Many gods have been done away with, but the individual himself stubbornly remains as a deity of considerable importance. He walks with some dignity and is the recipient of many little offerings. He is jealous of the worship due him, yet approached in the right spirit, he is ready to forgive those who may have offended him. Because of their status relative to his, some persons will find him contaminating while others will find they contaminate him, in either case finding that they must treat him with ritual care (Goffman, 1967: 95).

Santayana believed that life is a predicament. Were he alive today and had a chance to ponder the ideas presented in this book, he might want to add that every predicament contains its own special moral charge. Yet this is not the kind of morality we normally think of when the subject of morality comes up for discussion. For most Americans and Canadians see the morality connected with breaches of etiquette as very different from the morality connected with, say, murder, rape, or cheating on one's income tax.

All morality is expressed through the rules of the community, which serve as enduring guides for its social behavior. This much was said about etiquette in chapter 1. Still, when speaking of morality, we tend to speak of deviance of some sort, of murder, rape, or tax fraud and possibly of more tolerable offenses such as drunkenness, public nudity, or skid-row living (Stebbins, 1988: chapter 1). At least in North America, few violations of etiquette are regarded with such seriousness.

Be that as it may, violations of etiquette do have a moral quality, in part because they, too, are judged by particular community standards of right and wrong. This means everyday affairs are also moral affairs, and much more so than is commonly thought. Furthermore, deviant behavior is relatively rare when compared with breaches of etiquette which, as I have attempted to show throughout this book, are rather routine. Our community rules say it is wrong to offend someone, whether we intend to do so or not. Speaking philosophically, offenses in etiquette are no different from acts of tolerable or intolerable deviance; all are immoral. When speaking sociologically, however, we can see that people disdain the latter with considerably more force than the former, chiefly because they believe the latter more seriously threatens the social life of the community.

Let me clarify a common misconception by pointing out that, in one important sense, it is most inaccurate to treat custom as part of the body of rules of good manners we call etiquette. Custom is followed more or less unthinkingly, learned mostly in early life, and seen traditionally and unquestionably as inviolable. It follows that it is usually only the foreigners, the excentric, and the mentally disordered among us who are occasionally given to acting in uncostumary ways. By contrast, the perpetration of intended predicaments demonstrates how the rules of etiquette can be consciously disregarded or manipulated to serve personal advantage. Because of this flexibility, these rules can never be classified as unquestioned behavioral imperatives, as customary. They stand apart in a category of their own, a category that is, however, also distinct from the rules whose violation constitutes the more serious moral offenses we consider deviant.

What is more, predicaments and the everyday moral concepts from which they draw their meaning are moral incidents because they threaten the self-esteem of the people who have the misfortune to be involved in them. We maintain it is wrong to degrade the self-worth of others or, if we do such a thing, we presumably do it for "good" reasons, reasons justified as warranted punitive action. Still, it is possible that a certain proportion of intended predicaments are motivated by this very goal: punition. But intended or not, predicaments are punitive precisely because all except the most self-deprecating go to great lengths to avoid the threats to personal esteem inherent in them. As Walt Whitman put it, "nothing, but God, is greater to one than one's self is." This intense level of personal involvement in any given predicament substantially raises its moral loading.

All this justifies rather well the sociological study of etiquette and the ways we breach it. These violations are, after all, much more common than the rule violations we think of as deviant; etiquette is part of the core of everyday life, whereas deviance is, by its very nature, peripheral and unusual. Odd as it may seem, it is perhaps because of the commonplaceness of etiquette and its transgressions that sociological attention to this aspect of society has been so thin and sporadic. It would seem that, as their discipline evolved, many sociologists adopted the outlook of British novelist George Eliot: "If we had a keen vision of all that is ordinary in human life, it would be like hearing the grass grow or the squirrel's heart beat, and we should die of that roar which is the other side of silence." Santayana's proposition that life is a predicament - to which I believe this book lends considerable support - suggests, nonetheless, that Eliot (were he alive today) and many sociologists could profit from a reexamination of their assumptions about what is interesting and therefore worthy of careful study in everyday life.

References

Stebbins, Robert A.
　　1988　*Deviance: Tolerable Differences*. Toronto: McGraw-Hill Ryerson.

Index

About the Author

Robert A. Stebbins was born and raised in the United States, the same country where symbolic interactionism was pioneered and, in 1964 was granted his Ph.D. in sociology from the University of Minnesota, a longtime center of the perspective. Since then he has published numerous articles and chapters from the symbolic interactionist approach, seven of which are reprinted here. Of his fifteen books, *Commitment to Deviance: The Nonprofessional Criminal in the Community* (1976) and *Teachers and Meaning: Definitions of Classroom Situations* (1975) are the two that are the most closely aligned with this approach. His more recent books on amateurs and professionals, although based less exclusively on symbolic interactionism, are nonetheless significantly organized around some of its most important concepts, including career, self-conception, social world, and social interaction. Much of this work is summarized and elaborated in *Amateurs, Professionals, and Serious Leisure* (1992). He is presently a Professor in the Department of Sociology at The University of Calgary. He served as President of the Social Science Federation of Canada in 1991-1992, after having served as President of the Canadian Sociology and Anthropology Association in 1988-1989. He is currently studying the linguistic life-styles of those who inhabit the French Canadian communities outside Quebec.